INGLÉS
IDIOMÁTICO 1

Eugene E. Long • William Buckwald

EDITORIAL TRILLAS

México, Argentina, España
Colombia, Puerto Rico, Venezuela

Catalogación en la fuente

> Long, Eugene E.
> Inglés idiomático 1. -- 9a ed. -- México : Trillas, 2012
> (reimp. 2015).
> 256 p. : il. ; 23 cm.
> ISBN 978-607-17-1366-7
>
> 1. Inglés - Estudio y enseñanza - Estudiantes
> extranjeros. I. Buckwald, William. II. t
>
> D- 421'L245i   LC- PE1129.58'L6.5   23

La presentación y
disposición en conjunto de
INGLÉS IDIOMÁTICO 1
son propiedad del editor.
Ninguna parte de esta obra puede ser
reproducida o trasmitida, mediante ningún
sistema o método, electrónico o mecánico
(incluyendo el fotocopiado, la grabación
o cualquier sistema de recuperación y
almacenamiento de información),
sin consentimiento por escrito del editor

Derechos reservados
© AO, 2012, Editorial Trillas, S. A. de C. V.

División Administrativa,
Av. Río Churubusco 385,
Col. Gral. Pedro María Anaya,
C. P. 03340, México, D. F.
Tel. 56884233 FAX 56041364
churubusco@trillas.mx

División Logística,
Calzada de la Viga 1132,
C. P. 09439, México, D. F.
Tel. 56330995, FAX 56330870
laviga@trillas.mx

🞸 Tienda en línea
www.etrillas.mx

Miembro de la Cámara Nacional de
la Industria Editorial Reg. núm. 158

Segunda edición AO
⸎(MS, MT, MR)
Tercera edición MI
ISBN 978-968-24-3657-4
⸎(ML, MA, 1-7-MM, ME, 2-10-MX)
Cuarta edición MO
Quinta edición ES
⸎(ET, 5-10-ER, EI, EL, EA, EM, EE, EX)
Sexta edición EO
ISBN 968-24-0732-X
⸎(XS, XT, XR, XI, XL, XA, XM, XE, XX)
Séptima edición XO
ISBN 968-24-3245-X
Octava edición OS
ISBN 978-968-24-4000-7
⸎(OT, OR, OI, OL, OA, OM, OX, OO, SS
ST, SR, SI, SL, SA, SM, SE, SX, TS, TT)
Novena edición TR
ISBN 978-607-17-1366-7
(Octava publicada por
Editorial Trillas, S. A. de C. V.)
⸎(TI, TL)

Reimpresión, febrero 2015

Impreso en México
Printed in Mexico

Esta obra se imprimió
el 10 de febrero de 2015,
en los talleres de
Litográfica Ingramex, S. A. de C. V.

B 75 XW

ÍNDICE DE CONTENIDO

LESSON 1 — 9
El tiempo presente del verbo **be**
El uso de la partícula **not**

LESSON 2 — 16
Las contracciones afirmativas con los pronombres
La posición de los adjetivos en inglés

LESSON 3 — 22
Los artículos **a**, **an**
Los complementos con el artículo indefinido
El tiempo presente
To the teacher
Las preposiciones **to**, **in**

LESSON 4 — 29
Las preposiciones **on**, **at**, **from**
Hay - **there is (there's)** y **there are**
This, **this one**, **these**

LESSON 5 — 36
La preposición **of**
El verbo **like**
El auxiliar **can**
That, that one, **those**
Los adjetivos posesivos

LESSON 6 — 44
La palabra **home**
El gerundio
El tiempo presente progresivo

LESSON 7 54
    La preposición **for**
    El futuro idiomático

LESSON 8 64
    Los días de la semana
    El uso de las preposiciones **on**, **by**
    La forma posesiva
    El verbo **want**

LESSON 9 73
    El presente del verbo **do**
    Los auxiliares **do**, **does**
    El imperativo

LESSON 10 83
    La preposición **at** con tiempo y lugar
    To do, **to make**
    El verbo **have** (tener y haber)
    La expresión idiomática de necesidad
    La traducción de la partícula castellana a
    La traducción de **for** antes de un infinitivo
    Reglas de ortografía

LESSON 11 97
    El tiempo pasado del verbo **be**
    Los meses del año

LESSON 12 107
    El tiempo pasado progresivo
    El auxiliar **could**
    Los meses del año

LESSON 13 — 119

Había, hubo - **there was**, **there were**
Adverbios de frecuencia
El tiempo pasado del futuro idiomático

LESSON 14 — 132

El tiempo pasado de los verbos regulares
La pronunciación de la terminación **ed**
El pasado de los verbos irregulares

LESSON 15 — 145

El pasado del verbo **do**
El auxiliar **did**
El tiempo pasado de la expresión idiomática
   de necesidad

LESSON 16 — 157

Los pronombres objetivos
Like con los sustantivos y pronombres objetivos
El imperativo
El uso del gerundio con preposiciones
The dog in the manger

LESSON 17 — 172

Los pronombres posesivos
Much, **many**, **little**, **few**
To say, **to tell**
Preposiciones
The fox and the stork

LESSON 18   185
    Los pronombres y adjetivos indefinidos **some,**
        any, no, none
Some
Any, not... any
No, none
Something, anything, not... anything, nothing
Somebody (someone), anybody (anyone), not...
    anybody (anyone), nobody (no one)
Somewhere (some place), anywhere (any place),
    not... anywhere (any place), nowhere (no
    place)
Everything, everybody (everyone), everywhere
    (every place)
    Verbos y preposiciones
    The rabbit and the turtle

LESSON 19   207
    El equivalente de ¿no es verdad?
    To the teacher
    Las preposiciones al final de la oración
    Preposiciones
    The goose that laid the golden egg

LESSON 20   224
    Ortografía
    The crow and the pitcher

Vocabulary English-Spanish   241

VOCABULARY

1. **I** yo
2. **you** tú
3. **you** usted
4. **he** él
5. **she** ella
6. **it** ello (*cosa o animal*)
7. **we** nosotros
8. **you** ustedes
9. **they** ellos
10. **they** ellas
11. **they** ellos (*cosas o animales*)
12. **no** no
13. **to be** ser, estar

El tiempo presente del verbo **be**

Los infinitivos en inglés se forman colocando la partícula **to** antes del verbo. Así, **to be** forma un infinitivo con la partícula **to** antes del verbo **be**. Los infinitivos en castellano se forman con las terminaciones **ar**, **er**, **ir**. **To be** equivale a **ser** (terminación **er**) o estar (terminación **ar**), pues en inglés, a diferencia del castellano, **ser** y **estar** son un solo verbo.

En inglés no se puede sobreentender el pronombre como en castellano. Siempre hay que expresarlo.

Be – Afirmativo

I am	(yo)	soy, estoy
you are	(tú)	eres, estás
you are	(usted)	es, está
he is	(él)	es, está
she is	(ella)	es, está
it is	(*cosa o animal*)	es, está
we are	(nosotros)	somos, estamos
you are	(ustedes)	son, están
they are	(ellos)	son, están
they are	(ellas)	son, están
they are	(*cosas o animales*)	son, están

EXERCISE 1
Traduzca las siguientes frases.

1. yo soy
2. tú eres
3. usted es
4. él es
5. ella es
6. es (*cosa o animal*)
7. nosotros somos
8. ustedes son
9. ellos son
10. ellas son
11. yo estoy
12. tú estás
13. usted está
14. él está
15. ella está
16. estamos
17. ustedes están
18. ellos están
19. ellas están
20. eres
21. él está
22. soy
23. ellos son
24. ella está
25. nosotros estamos
26. es (*cosa o animal*)
27. tú estás
28. nosotros somos
29. ustedes están
30. están (*cosas o animales*)

El uso de la partícula not

La palabra **not** se usa en inglés para negar, pero siempre acompañada de algún verbo. En general se coloca inmediatamente después del verbo. En las siguientes frases **I am not**, **he is not**, **they are not**, **we are not**, nótese que el verbo y la partícula **not** se escriben como dos palabras separadas. Esto es muy común en el inglés escrito. En una conversación, sin embargo, el verbo y la partícula **not** se juntan para formar una contracción, la que se usa con frecuencia y casi sin excepción. En la primera persona del singular la contracción es **I'm not**. La contracción de **is not** es **isn't** y de **are not**, **aren't**.

Be – Negativo

I'm not	(yo)	no soy, no estoy
you aren't	(tú)	no eres, no estás
you aren't	(usted)	no es, no está
he isn't	(él)	no es, no está
she isn't	(ella)	no es, no está
it isn't	(*cosa o animal*)	no es, no está
we aren't	(nosotros)	no somos, no estamos
you aren't	(ustedes)	no son, no están
they aren't	(ellos)	no son, no están
they aren't	(ellas)	no son, no están
they aren't	(*cosas o animales*)	no son, no están

EXERCISE 2
Traduzca las siguientes frases.

1. no soy
2. tú no eres
3. usted no es
4. él no es
5. ella no es
6. no es (*cosa o animal*)
7. no somos
8. ustedes no son
9. ellos no son
10. ellas no son

11. yo no estoy
12. tú no estás
13. usted no está
14. él no está
15. ella no está
16. no está (*cosa o animal*)
17. nosotros no estamos
18. ustedes no están
19. ellos no están
20. ellas no están

21. tú no eres
22. él no es
23. ellas no están
24. yo no estoy
25. ustedes no están
26. ella no es
27. yo no estoy
28. usted no está
29. tú no estás
30. él no está

EXERCISE 3
Cambie al negativo.

1. he is
2. we are
3. they are
4. I am
5. she is
6. you are
7. I am
8. it is

9. you are
10. we are
11. he is
12. they are
13. she is
14. I am
15. it is
16. we are

Be – **Interrogativo**

La forma interrogativa del verbo **be** se forma colocando el verbo antes del sustantivo o pronombre.

am I?	¿soy yo? ¿estoy yo?
are you?	¿eres tú? ¿estás tú?
are you?	¿es usted? ¿está usted?
is he?	¿es él? ¿está él?
is she?	¿es ella? ¿está ella?
is it?	¿es? (*cosa o animal*) ¿está? (*cosa o animal*)
are we?	¿somos nosotros? ¿estamos nosotros?
are you?	¿son ustedes? ¿están ustedes?

> **are they?** ¿son ellos? ¿están ellos?
> **are they?** ¿son ellas? ¿están ellas?
> **are they?** ¿son? (*cosas o animales*) ¿están? (*cosas o animales*)

EXERCISE 4
Traduzca las siguientes frases.

1. ¿soy?
2. ¿eres?
3. ¿es usted?
4. ¿es él?
5. ¿es ella?
6. ¿es? (*cosa o animal*)
7. ¿somos?
8. ¿son ustedes?
9. ¿son ellos?
10. ¿son ellas?
11. ¿estoy?
12. ¿estás?
13. ¿está usted?
14. ¿está él?
15. ¿está ella?
16. ¿está? (*cosa o animal*)
17. ¿estamos?
18. ¿están ustedes?
19. ¿están ellos?
20. ¿están ellas?
21. ¿eres?
22. ¿está él?
23. ¿son ellos?
24. ¿es ella?
25. ¿somos?
26. ¿están ustedes?
27. ¿soy?
28. ¿es usted?
29. ¿estoy?
30. ¿estás?

EXERCISE 5
Cambie al negativo y al interrogativo.

1. he is
2. we are
3. they are
4. I am
5. she is
6. you are
7. I am
8. it is
9. you are
10. we are
11. he is
12. they are
13. she is
14. I am
15. it is
16. he is

Be - Interrogativo negativo

La forma interrogativa negativa del verbo **be** se construye colocando la contracción del negativo antes del sustantivo o pronombre. Fíjese que en la primera persona singular no es posible ninguna contracción con **am** y **not**.

am I not?	¿no soy yo? ¿no estoy yo?
aren't you?	¿no eres tú? ¿no estás tú?
aren't you?	¿no es usted? ¿no está usted?
isn't he?	¿no es él? ¿no está él?
isn't she?	¿no es ella? ¿no está ella?
isn't it?	¿no es? (*cosa o animal*) ¿no está? (*cosa o animal*)
aren't we?	¿no somos nosotros? ¿no estamos nosotros?
aren't you?	¿no son ustedes? ¿no están ustedes?
aren't they?	¿no son ellos? ¿no están ellos?
aren't they?	¿no son ellas? ¿no están ellas?
aren't they?	¿no son? (*cosas o animales*)
	¿no están? (*cosas o animales*)

EXERCISE 6
Traduzca las siguientes frases.

1. ¿no soy yo?
2. ¿no eres tú?
3. ¿no es usted?
4. ¿no es él?
5. ¿no es ella?
6. ¿no es? (*cosa o animal*)
7. ¿no somos nosotros?
8. ¿no son ustedes?
9. ¿no son ellos?
10. ¿no son ellas?
11. ¿no estoy yo?
12. ¿no estás tú?
13. ¿no está usted?
14. ¿no está él?
15. ¿no está ella?
16. ¿no está? (*cosa o animal*)
17. ¿no estamos nosotros?
18. ¿no están ustedes?
19. ¿no están ellos?
20. ¿no están ellas?
21. ¿no está él?
22. ¿no son? (*cosas o animales*)
23. ¿no es ella?
24. ¿no somos?

25. ¿no están ustedes?
26. ¿no soy yo?
27. ¿no están? (*cosas o animales*)
28. ¿no es usted?
29. ¿no estoy yo?
30. ¿no estás?

EXERCISE 7
Cambie al negativo, interrogativo e interrogativo negativo.

1. he is
2. we are
3. they are
4. I am
5. she is
6. you are
7. I am
8. it is
9. you are
10. we are
11. he is
12. they are
13. she is
14. I am
15. it is
16. we are

EXERCISE 8
Traduzca las siguientes frases.

1. él es
2. él no es
3. ¿es él?
4. ¿no es él?
5. tú estás
6. tú no estás
7. ¿estás tú?
8. ¿no estás?
9. somos
10. nosotros no somos
11. ¿somos nosotros?
12. ¿no somos nosotros?
13. ellos están
14. ellos no están
15. ¿están ellos?
16. ¿no están ellos?
17. yo soy
18. yo no soy
19. ¿soy yo?
20. ¿no soy yo?
21. es (*cosa o animal*)
22. no es (*cosa o animal*)
23. ¿es? (*cosa o animal*)
24. ¿no es? (*cosa o animal*)
25. ella está
26. ella no está
27. ¿está ella?
28. ¿no está ella?
29. son (*cosas o animales*)
30. no son (*cosas o animales*)
31. ¿son? (*cosas o animales*)
32. ¿no son? (*cosas o animales*)

Lesson 2

VOCABULARY

1. **the** el, la, los, las
2. **yes** sí
3. **boy** niño, muchacho
4. **girl** niña, muchacha
5. **man** hombre
6. **woman** mujer
7. **house** casa
8. **car** coche
9. **big** grande, gran
10. **little** pequeño, chico (*tamaño*)
    small pequeño, chico (*cantidad*)
11. **old** viejo, grande (*edad*)
12. **young** joven
13. **new** nuevo
14. **red** rojo
15. **green** verde
16. **American** estadounidense
17. **Mexican** mexicano
18. **where** dónde, donde
19. **apple** manzana
20. **sweet** (*adj.*) dulce
21. **desk** escritorio
22. **brown** color café
23. **idiom** modismo

IDIOMS

1. hello hola
2. good-bye adiós
3. good morning buenos días
4. good afternoon buenas tardes
5. good evening (*para saludar*) buenas noches
6. good night (*para despedirse*) buenas noches
7. the young man (boy) el joven
   the young woman (girl) la joven
8. the old man el anciano
   the old woman la anciana

* **Idiom**. Expresión que no puede entenderse a partir de los significados de las palabras que la componen, y que tiene un sentido establecido por el uso.

LESSON 2

EXERCISE 1
Traduzca las siguientes oraciones y practique leyéndolas.

1. I am Mexican.
2. You are American.
3. He is old.
4. She is young.
5. It is new.
6. We are Mexican.
7. They are American.
8. I'm not Mexican.
9. You aren't American.
10. He isn't old.
11. She isn't young.
12. It isn't new.
13. We aren't Mexican.
14. They aren't American.
15. Where are they?
16. Where is he?
17. Are you Mexican?
18. Aren't you American?
19. Isn't he young?
20. Are they old?
21. Are you American?
22. Where are they?
23. They are red.
24. Aren't they sweet?

Las contracciones afirmativas con los pronombres

Fíjese en las contracciones afirmativas con los pronombres. Éstas solamente se pueden usar cuando el verbo se complementa. En oraciones negativas las contracciones se pueden usar haya o no complemento.

I'm Mexican.	Soy mexicano.
You're American.	Eres estadounidense.
You're young.	Usted es joven.
He's old.	Él es viejo.
She's little.	Ella es pequeña.
It's sweet.	Está dulce.
We're American.	Somos estadounidenses.
You're Mexican.	Ustedes son mexicanos.
They're boys.	Son muchachos.
They're girls.	Son muchachas.
They're big.	Están grandes.

La posición de los adjetivos en inglés

En inglés los adjetivos se colocan antes de los sustantivos. Los adjetivos en inglés nunca cambian de forma. No tienen ni singular ni plural, ni son masculinos ni femeninos como en castellano. Estudie usted las siguientes frases. Fíjese en la posición de los adjetivos **red**, **big**, **little** en las expresiones, y note que no cambian de forma. Puesto que el artículo **the** es adjetivo, tampoco sufre cambio alguno.

1. **the big house** — la casa grande
2. **the big houses** — las casas grandes
3. **the red car** — el coche rojo
4. **the red cars** — los coches rojos
5. **the little girl** — la muchacha (niña) pequeña
6. **the little boys** — los muchachos (niños) pequeños

EXERCISE 2

Traduzca al inglés.

1. el anciano
2. la manzana grande
3. los escritorios nuevos
4. el joven
5. el coche pequeño
6. el coche viejo
7. la joven
8. el señor
9. la señorita

Traduzca al castellano.

1. The new car is red.
2. The old car is green.
3. Where are the little girls?
4. The apple is sweet.
5. Where is the young woman?
6. Where are the small cars?

EXERCISE 3

Traduzca las siguientes oraciones. Cámbielas al negativo, interrogativo e interrogativo negativo.

1. He's young.
2. It's new.
3. She's old.
4. They're big.
5. You're Mexican.
6. We're little.
7. I'm young.
8. It's sweet.

EXERCISE 4

Traduzca las siguientes oraciones. Cámbielas al negativo, interrogativo e interrogativo negativo.

1. The desk is brown.
2. The cars are new.
3. The woman is old.
4. The apples are red.
5. The girl is Mexican.
6. The cars are old.
7. The Mexican girls are little.
8. The house is big.

EXERCISE 5

Traduzca las siguientes oraciones. Cámbielas al negativo, interrogativo e interrogativo negativo.

1. The young man is big.
2. The new cars are red.
3. The little house is green.
4. The Mexican boy is big.
5. The American girl is little.
6. The small houses are old.
7. The American girls are young.
8. The big desk is old.
9. The red apple is sweet.

EXERCISE 6

Llene los espacios con **is** *o* **are**, *según el caso, y traduzca.*

1. The apples _____ small.
2. The girls _____ Mexican.
3. He _____ young.
4. The new cars _____ green.
5. We _____ American boys.
6. The girls _____ little.
7. It _____ red.
8. They _____ young girls.
9. The big cars _____ red.
10. The Mexican man _____ old.

EXERCISE 7

Traduzca las siguientes oraciones y practique leyéndolas.

1. The boy is little.
2. The boy isn't little.
3. Is the boy little?
4. Isn't the boy little?
5. Where's the boy?
6. The boys are young.
7. The boys aren't young.
8. Are the boys young?
9. Aren't the boys young?
10. The man is American.
11. The man isn't American.
12. Is the man American?
13. Isn't the man American?
14. Where's the man?
15. The big house is new.
16. The big house isn't new.
17. Is the big house new?
18. Isn't the big house new?
19. It's brown.
20. It isn't brown.
21. Is it brown?
22. Isn't it brown?

EXERCISE 8
Lea y traduzca estas oraciones.

1. The brown desk is new.
2. The American girls aren't little.
3. Is the new car red?
4. No, the new car isn't red. It's green.
5. Where is the little boy?
6. Isn't the young woman Mexican?
7. Are the houses big? Yes, they're big.
8. They aren't little boys. They're young girls.
9. Where are the American girls?
10. Aren't the apples sweet?

EXERCISE 9
Escriba en inglés.

1. ¿Es usted mexicano?
2. No, no soy mexicano. Soy estadounidense.
3. Los muchachos son jóvenes.
4. Las muchachas grandes no son mexicanas.
5. Las casas son rojas.
6. ¿Dónde está el niño pequeño?
7. ¿No es rojo el coche nuevo?
8. Sí, el coche nuevo es rojo.
9. ¿Dónde están las muchachas estadounidenses?
10. El no es viejo. Es joven.

Lesson 3

VOCABULARY

1. **to go** ir
2. **to come** venir; llegar
3. **to work** trabajar
4. **a, an** un, una
5. **and** y, e
6. **to** a
7. **in** en, dentro de
8. **with** con
9. **my** mi, mis
10. **too** también
11. **here** acá, aquí
12. **table** mesa
13. **telephone** teléfono
    phone teléfono
14. **office** oficina
15. **school** escuela
16. **movie** película
17. **father** padre, papá
18. **mother** madre, mamá
19. **brother** hermano
20. **sister** hermana
21. **Spanish** español
22. **teacher** profesor, maestro

IDIOMS

1. **Mr. Hunt** el Sr. Hunt
2. **Mrs. Hunt** la Sra. Hunt
3. **Miss Hunt** la señorita. Hunt
4. **Mr. and Mrs. Hunt** los señores Hunt
   (**Mr., Mrs., Miss** se emplean solamente con los nombres y los apellidos. El artículo no se usa con estas palabras.)

5. **He goes to the movies.** Él va al cine.
6. **every day** todos los días
7. **Thank you.** Gracias.
8. **You're welcome.** De nada, por nada.

EXERCISE 1

Traduzca las siguientes oraciones y practique leyéndolas.

1. I'm in the office.
2. Am I in the office?
3. I'm not in the office.
4. Am I not in the office?
5. He's my brother.
6. The boy is American.
7. John isn't American.
8. Is John American?
9. She's Mexican.
10. She isn't Mexican.
11. My father is here.
12. My father isn't here.
13. Is Mary here?
14. Isn't Mary here?
15. Where is Mary?
16. She's here.

Los artículos a, an

El artículo **a** se emplea antes de palabras que empiezan con consonante. El artículo **an** se emplea antes de palabras que empiezan con vocal. Ejemplos: **an American girl, an office, a boy, a Mexican man.**

EXERCISE 2

*Llene los espacios con **a** o **an** y traduzca.*

1. _____ big desk
2. _____ red apple
3. _____ Mexican woman
4. _____ American woman
5. _____ new office
6. _____ office
7. _____ old car
8. _____ young boy

Los complementos con el artículo indefinido

En inglés, los complementos en singular que se pueden contar llevan el artículo indefinido antes del sustantivo. Los complementos en plural no van precedidos de artículo indefinido.

	He's a little boy.	Él es (un) muchachito.
	I'm a teacher.	Soy profesor.
	It's a big car.	Es (un) coche grande.
pero:	It's water. (*No se puede contar el agua.*)	Es agua.
	They're little boys.	Son muchachitos.
	We're teachers.	Somos profesores.
	They're big cars.	Son coches grandes.

EXERCISE 3
Traduzca al inglés.

1. Es (un) coche grande.
2. ¿Es (una) casa chica?
3. Ella no es (una) muchacha joven.
4. ¿Es (una) escuela grande?
5. Soy (un) profesor.
6. Somos profesores.
7. Es (un) coche nuevo.
8. ¿No es (un) muchacho chico?
9. No son muchachos chicos.
10. Es (un) padre.

EXERCISE 4
Traduzca las siguientes oraciones. Cámbielas al negativo, interrogativo e interrogativo negativo.

1. A young girl is here.
2. She's a young girl.
3. John is an American boy.
4. An American boy is here.
5. Mr. Green is a young man.
6. Mr. Smith is an old man.
7. He's a Mexican boy.
8. An apple is red.
9. A big table is in the house.
10. An American woman is in the office.

El tiempo presente

Para conjugar cualquier verbo en el afirmativo del presente (menos los verbos **be** y **have**), se quita la partícula **to** del infinitivo y se antepone el pronombre.

Con los pronombres de la tercera persona del singular, o sea **he, she, it**, y con un sustantivo usado en singular como **boy, girl, house** siempre se añade una **s** al verbo.

Este tiempo se usa para representar una acción habitual o un estado o un hecho.

I come	(yo) vengo	**we come**	(nosotros) venimos
you come	(tú) vienes	**you come**	(ustedes) vienen
you come	(usted) viene	**they come**	(ellos) vienen
he comes	(él) viene	**they come**	(ellas) vienen
she comes	(ella) viene	**they come**	(*cosas o animales*)
it comes	(*cosa o animal*) viene		vienen

To the teacher

The exercises in each lesson marked as **Práctica verbal** are to be used as a verb conjugation study. Each exercise of this type will consist of a group of short sentences that will serve as a model for all the verb tenses and constructions with which the students have become familiar.

The sentences should be: 1) translated into Spanish so the student will know exactly what he is repeating in English; 2) read in English one at a time by the teacher with emphasis placed on pronunciation and repeated in chorus by the students; 3) read in chorus by the students until they have mastered the verb tenses, construction, and word order.

LESSON 3

EXERCISE 5
Práctica verbal

1. I go to school.
2. You go to school.
3. He goes to school.
4. She goes to school.
5. John goes to school.
6. We go to school.
7. You go to school.
8. They go to school.
9. Robert goes to school.
10. My sister goes to school.
11. Mr. Hunt goes to school.
12. Miss Hunt goes to school.
13. John and I go to school.
14. Mrs. Hunt and I go to school.
15. John and Mary go to school.
16. The boys go to school.
17. The girls go to school too.
18. My brothers go to school too.

EXERCISE 6
Práctica verbal. *Repita el ejercicio 5, usando formas de los verbos* **come** *(to school) y* **work** *(in an office).*

Las preposiciones to, in

La preposición **to** (a) se usa después de los verbos que indican movimiento.

La preposición **in** (en, dentro de) se usa para indicar que se está dentro de cierto lugar.

Estudie las siguientes frases: **to school, to the office, to the movies, in the office, in the house, in school.**

EXERCISE 7
Llene los espacios con la preposición correcta y traduzca.

1. John goes (a) _____ school.
2. Robert is (en) _____ the house.
3. The table is (en) _____ the office.
4. My mother goes (a) _____ the office.
5. John comes (a) _____ the office with Mr. Brown.

6. Mary is (en) _____ school.
7. The boys are (en) _____ the car.
8. My sister is (en) _____ the house.
9. My brother goes (a) _____ the movies every day.
10. My brothers are (en) _____ the office.

EXERCISE 8
Lea y traduzca estas oraciones.

1. John and Robert go to school with Mary.
2. He works in a big office.
3. Mr. and Mrs. Hunt come to the office.
4. My mother works in the house.
5. My sister works in the house too.
6. My father is American, and my mother is Mexican.
7. Are the apples sweet?
8. No, the desk isn't new.
9. Where are the American boys and girls?
10. The American girls are with my sister.
11. Isn't Robert with my sister too?
12. Mary is a little girl, and John is a little boy.

EXERCISE 9
Escriba en inglés.

1. Mi hermano pequeño va a la escuela.
2. Mi hermana va a la escuela todos los días.
3. ¿Es usted mexicano? Sí, yo soy mexicano.
4. ¿Están las muchachas con Roberto? No, están en la casa.
5. Juan está con mi mamá también.
6. Mis hermanos no son pequeños. Son grandes.
7. Mis hermanos trabajan en una oficina, y mi padre trabaja en una oficina también.
8. ¿Dónde están los muchachos estadounidenses?
9. La señorita Davis no está en la escuela.
10. El señor Hunt va al cine. La señora Hunt va al cine también.

EXERCISE 10
Dictado

1. Robert is here too.
2. My father comes to the office every day.
3. My father and mother are here.
4. Where are the Mexican boys?
5. Aren't you Mexican? No, I'm American.
6. Miss Taylor works in a big office.
7. John goes to school in a car.
8. We go to school too.
9. My sisters go to the movies every day.
10. Is the man here?

EXERCISE 11
Conversación. *Conteste cada pregunta en afirmativo y en negativo.*

1. Are you Mexican?
2. Isn't the boy here?
3. Are the girls in the house?
4. Aren't the boys brothers?
5. Is the boy little?
6. Is Robert an American?
7. Are the boys in the car?
8. Isn't the little boy Mexican?
9. Aren't the girls with John?
10. Are they sisters?
11. Are they brothers?
12. Is the man American?
13. Isn't Robert with Mr. Hunt?
14. Is Mary with Miss Hunt?
15. Is John a big boy?

Lesson 4

VOCABULARY

1. **to read** leer
2. **to say** decir
3. **to write** escribir
4. **to use** usar
5. **to take** llevar, tomar
6. **on** en, sobre
7. **at** en
8. **from** de
9. **this** este, esta, esto
10. **this one** éste, ésta
11. **these** estos, estas; éstos, éstas
12. **how** cómo
13. **how many** cuántos
14. **good** bueno
15. **well** bien
16. **book** libro
17. **notebook** cuaderno
18. **pencil** lápiz
19. **pen** pluma
20. **letter** carta; letra
21. **there is, there are** hay (*singular, plural*)
    is there?, are there? ¿hay? (*singular, plural*)
22. **one** (1), **two** (2), **three** (3), **four** (4), **five** (5)

IDIOMS

1. **How are you?** ¿Cómo está usted.?
2. **Fine, thank you.** Bien, gracias.
3. **What's your name?** ¿Cómo se llama?
   My name is John. Me llamo Juan.
4. **first name** nombre de pila
5. **last name** apellido
6. **He's at home.** Él está en casa.

LESSON 4

EXERCICE 1
Traduzca las siguientes oraciones y practique leyéndolas.

1. Where are you?
2. How are you?
3. He's at home.
4. He isn't at home.
5. Is she at home?
6. Isn't she at home?
7. We're in school.
8. We aren't in school.
9. Is Mary in school?
10. Isn't Mary in school?
11. You're an American.
12. You aren't an American.
13. Are they Americans?
14. Aren't they Americans?
15. Where's the car?
16. Where are the notebooks?
17. The boys go to school.
18. The girls go to school too.
19. Where is the telephone?
20. It's in the office.
21. Robert goes to school.
22. My sister goes to school.
23. They come to school.
24. I come to school too.
25. Mr. Hunt works in an office.

Las preposiciones on, at, from

La preposición **on** (en, sobre) indica estar sobre una superficie.
La preposición **at** (en) indica un lugar determinado.
La preposición **from** (de) indica procedencia u origen.
Estudie las siguientes frases: **on the table, on the desk, on Reforma, at the movies, at home, at school, at 5 Reforma, from the office, from home, from school, from the movies.**

EXERCISE 2
Llene los espacios con la preposición correcta y traduzca.

1. My father is (en) _____ home.
2. My little brothers are (en) _____ school.
3. My father works (en) _____ an office.
4. My sister comes (de) _____ school.
5. The letter is (sobre) _____ the table.
6. The pencil is (en) _____ the notebook.

7. John is (en) _____ the movies.
8. I come (de) _____ home.
9. My sister goes (a) _____ school.
10. This pen is (sobre) _____ the desk.
11. I work (en) _____ Insurgentes.
12. I work (en) _____ 4 Insurgentes.

EXERCISE 3
Traduzca las siguientes oraciones. Cámbielas al negativo, interrogativo e interrogativo negativo.

1. The table is green.
2. My first name is John.
3. My last name is Hunt.
4. The woman is in the house.
5. My father is in the office.
6. My brothers are at school.
7. The girl is in the house.
8. A man is in the office.
9. A book is on the desk.
10. My sisters are at the movies.

Hay - there is (there's) y there are

Hay equivale a **there is** (**there's**) y **there are**. **There is** (**there's**) es singular y **there are** es plural. **Is there** y **are there** son las formas interrogativas. **There isn't** y **there aren't** son las formas negativas.

EXERCISE 4
Llene los espacios con **there is** *(***there's***) o* **there are**, **is there** *o* **are there**, **there isn't** *o* **there aren't** *y traduzca.*

1. _____ an apple on the desk.
2. _____ two boys with my brothers.
3. How many girls _____ in the house?
4. _____ an American woman here.

LESSON 4

5. _____ (*negativo*) two green pencils.
6. How many green pencils _____?
7. How many green pens _____ on the table?
8. _____ (*negativo*) a telephone in the office.
9. _____ four red pencils and five green pens.
10. _____ three boys and two girls.

EXERCISE 5

Traduzca las siguientes oraciones y practique leyéndolas.

1. There's a boy here.
2. There isn't a boy here.
3. Is there a girl here?
4. Isn't there a girl here?
5. There are three books here.
6. How many books are there?
7. There aren't five notebooks here.
8. Is there a pencil on the desk?

This, this one, these

Se emplea el adjetivo **this** (este, esta) con sustantivo en singular y el pronombre **this one** (éste, ésta) al referirse a un sustantivo ya mencionado o sobreentendido.

La palabra **these** (estos, estas; éstos, éstas) se emplea, tanto en inglés como en castellano, con o sin sustantivo.

> **This** book is red and **this one** is green.
> **Este** libro es rojo y **éste** es verde.
>
> **These** books are red and **these** are green.
> **Estos** libros son rojos y **éstos** son verdes.

EXERCISE 6
Llene los espacios con **this, this one** *(singular)* o **these** *(plural) y traduzca.*

1. _____ man is my father.
2. _____ boys are my brothers.
3. _____ girls go to school.
4. _____ boys use _____ book. I use _____ too.
5. _____ girl isn't my sister.
6. _____ pencil is red, and _____ is green.
7. John takes _____ red books to school. I take _____.
8. I use _____ pencils in the office.
9. _____ boys are good. _____ isn't.
10. _____ woman reads _____ good books.

EXERCISE 7
Práctica verbal

1. I read a book.
2. You read a book.
3. He reads a book.
4. John reads a letter.
5. The boy reads too.
6. Miss Hunt reads too.
7. Robert reads too.
8. He reads at home.
9. She reads at home.
10. They read at home.
11. I read in school.
12. John reads in school.
13. This boy reads.
14. This girl reads too.
15. These boys read.
16. These boys read too.
17. Mr. and Mrs. Hunt read.
18. Miss Taylor reads too.
19. John and Robert read.
20. My brother reads too.

EXERCISE 8

Práctica verbal. *Repita el ejercicio 7, usando las formas de los verbos* **write** *(a letter),* **say** *(this),* **use** *(a notebook),* **take** *(this book).*

EXERCISE 9
Lea y traduzca estas oraciones.

1. There are five boys and four girls in this school.
2. Robert takes two books to school.
3. Sara is my first name. My last name is Taylor.
4. Mrs. Taylor says, "How are you?"
5. How many letters are there on this table?
6. There aren't two notebooks here.
7. There isn't a telephone in the office.
8. Aren't there boys in this school?
9. "Thank you", says John. "You' re welcome", says Robert and Mary.
10. We use books and pencils at school, and they use pencils and pens at the office.

EXERCISE 10
Escriba en inglés.

1. Este señor lee un buen libro.
2. ¿Cuántos cuadernos hay sobre el escritorio?
3. Yo llevo mi libro a la escuela todos los días.
4. Estas muchachas usan cuadernos, lápices y plumas en la oficina.
5. Me llamo Henry Brown.
6. ¿Cómo está usted? Bien, gracias.
7. Hay una señorita estadounidense aquí.
8. Hay tres teléfonos en la oficina.
9. ¿Hay dos cartas sobre la mesa?
10. Mi apellido es Johnson.

EXERCISE 11
Dictado

1. "How are you?" says Mary.
2. "Fine, thank you," say John and Robert.
3. There aren't four boys in the house.
4. How many telephones are there in the office?
5. This boy takes a book to school.
6. These girls go to school in a car.
7. How many girls work in the office?
8. My name is Robert Brown.
9. Isn't there a pencil in this notebook?
10. Aren't there three notebooks on the desk?

EXERCISE 12
Conversación. *Conteste las siguientes preguntas.*

1. How are you?
2. What's your name?
3. How many pencils are there on the desk?
4. How many phones are there in the office?

Conteste las siguiente preguntas en afirmativo y negativo.

5. Is there a notebook on the desk?
6. Aren't there Mexican boys here?
7. Aren't there girls in school?
8. Aren't there desks in the office?
9. Is there an American boy here?
10. Are there American girls here?
11. Are you from Mexico?
12. Are the girls at home?
13. Is this book red?
14. Is this one green?
15. Are these cars American?

Lesson 5

VOCABULARY

1. **to live** vivir
2. **to eat** comer
3. **to help** ayudar
4. **to bring** traer
5. **to like** gustar; simpatizar
6. **can** poder
7. **candy** (*sing.*) dulces, caramelo
8. **of** de
9. **very** muy
10. **many** muchos
11. **some** alguno(s)
12. **everything** todo, todas las cosas
13. **that** ese, esa, eso; aquel, aquella, aquello
14. **that one** ése, ésa; aquél, aquélla
15. **those** esos, esas; aquellos, aquellas; ésos, ésas; aquéllos, aquéllas
16. **the United States** (los) Estados Unidos
17. **street** calle
18. **city** ciudad
19. **park** parque; jardín
20. **dinner** la comida principal
21. **six** (6), **seven** (7), **eight** (8), **nine** (9), **ten** (10)

IDIOMS

1. **Here it is.** Aquí está.
2. **It's very big.** Es muy grande.
3. **It's very little.** Es muy chico.
4. **There's room.** Hay lugar.
   There's no room. No hay lugar.

5. **He's very nice.** Él es muy simpático (agradable).
6. **The car is very nice.** El coche es muy bonito.
7. **He can read, write, etc.** Él sabe leer, escribir, etc.
8. **all the boys, girls, books, etc.** todos los muchachos, muchachas, libros, etc.

EXERCISE 1
Traduzca las siguientes oraciones y practique leyéndolas.

1. There's a girl here.
2. There isn't a boy here.
3. Are there many cars?
4. How many cars are there?
5. Is there a telephone here?
6. No, there isn't.
7. Aren't there ten letters?
8. No, there are eight.
9. How many notebooks are there?
10. There are five.
11. You write many letters.
12. He uses a brown pen.
13. I use this one.
14. He uses that one.
15. He says this.
16. He says that.
17. Mr. Martin says yes.
18. Mrs. Martin says no.
19. I write every day.
20. He writes every day too.
21. He reads English.
22. I read English too.
23. John reads English.
24. Mary reads English too.

La preposición of

La preposición **of** (de) indica parte de algo o pertenencia. Estudie estas frases: **some of the boys**, **many of the girls**.

EXERCISE 2
Llene los espacios con la preposición correcta y traduzca.

1. I live (en) _____ 9 Harvey Street.
2. I live (en) _____ a very big city.
3. Alice goes (a) _____ the park every day.
4. The boys go (a) _____ the movies.
5. Some (de) _____ the boys live (en) _____ the city.

LESSON 5

6. Many (de) _____ the girls live (en) _____ the United States.
7. These girls live (en) _____ my street.
8. My brother works (en) _____ an office.
9. We bring the books (a) _____ school.
10. Everything is (en) _____ the table.

El verbo like

El verbo **like** se conjuga igual que todos los otros verbos. La forma verbal que se usa después de éste será el infinitivo con la partícula **to**. Estudie las siguientes oraciones:

I like **to** help.	Me gusta ayudar.
You like **to** read.	A ti te gusta leer.
He likes **to** work.	A él le gusta trabajar.
John likes **to** work.	A Juan le gusta trabajar.
It (*animal*) likes **to** eat.	Le gusta comer.
We like **to** write.	Nos gusta escribir.
You like candy.	A ustedes les gustan los dulces.
They like the movie.	A ellos les gusta la película.
My brothers like Mary.	A mis hermanos les simpatiza María.

El auxiliar can

La palabra **can** es auxiliar. Un auxiliar es el que se usa con otro verbo para formar tiempos o modos. La forma del verbo que se usa después de **can** siempre es el infinitivo sin la partícula **to**. En oraciones interrogativas el auxiliar siempre se coloca antes del sustantivo o del pronombre. La negación del auxiliar **can** es **can not**. En conversación se usa la contracción **can't**. Por ser **can** un auxiliar, la tercera persona singular no termina en **s**. Estudie las siguientes frases:

I can go	puedo ir
I can't go	no puedo ir
you can come	puedes venir
you can't come	no puedes venir
he can help	él puede ayudar
he can't help	él no puede ayudar

Fíjese en la forma que se usa para construir el interrogativo o interrogativo negativo: auxiliar, sustantivo o pronombre, verbo.

Auxiliar	Sustantivo o pronombre	Verbo
Can	I	come?
¿Puedo	(yo)	venir?
(Where) can	the boy	go?
¿(Dónde) puede	el muchacho	ir?
Can't	they	help?
¿No pueden	ellos	ayudar?

EXERCISE 3
Traduzca las siguientes oraciones y practique leyéndolas.

1. I like to go to school.
2. You like to come too.
3. He likes to help.
4. She likes to help too.
5. We like to work.
6. You like to say that.
7. They like to read.
8. John likes the car.
9. My sister likes John.
10. My mother likes candy.
11. I can go every day.
12. I can't go every day.
13. Can I go every day?
14. Can't I go every day?
15. Where can I go?
16. You can help Alice.
17. You can't help Alice.
18. Can you help Alice?
19. Can't you help Alice?
20. He can eat apples.
21. He can't eat apples.
22. Can he eat apples?
23. How many apples can he eat?
24. Can't he eat apples every day?

LESSON 5

That, that one, those

Se emplea el adjetivo **that** (ese, esa; aquel, aquella) con sustantivo en singular y el pronombre **that one** (ése, ésa; aquél, aquélla) al referirse a un sustantivo ya mencionado o sobreentendido.

La palabra **those** (esos, esas; aquellos, aquellas; ésos, ésas; aquéllos, aquéllas) se emplea en inglés, con o sin sustantivo.

> **That** boy is Mexican and **that one** is American.
> **Ese** muchacho es mexicano y **aquél** es estadounidense.
>
> **Those** boys are Mexican and **those** are American.
> **Esos** muchachos son mexicanos y **aquéllos** son estadounidenses.

EXERCISE 4
Llene los espacios con **that, that one** *(singular) o* **those** *(plural) y traduzca.*

1. _____ girls live in Mexico.
2. _____ boy lives in the city.
3. _____ man lives at 10 Grant Street.
4. _____ girls aren't my sisters. _____ is.
5. I like to help _____ girl.
6. You like _____ movie.
7. _____ boys can help Mrs. Grant.
8. Can you go to _____ park?
9. Can't you live on _____ street?
10. He works in _____ city.
11. _____ books are red. _____ is green.

Los adjetivos posesivos

Los adjetivos posesivos en inglés, como otros adjetivos, no son ni singulares ni plurales. Puesto que son adjetivos, se colocarán antes de los sustantivos. Aprenda lo siguiente:

my	mi, mis
your	tu, tus
your	su, sus (de usted o de ustedes)
his	su, sus (de él)
her	su, sus (de ella)
its	su (de una cosa)
our	nuestro(s), nuestra(s)
their	su, sus (de ellos o de ellas)

EXERCISE 5
Llene los espacios con los adjetivos posesivos y traduzca.

1. Mother likes (su, *de ella*) _____ new house.
2. I bring (mi) _____ book.
3. Robert goes to school with (su, *de él*) _____ brother.
4. They help (su, *de ellos*) _____ mother.
5. We take (nuestros) _____ pencils.
6. You read (su, *de usted*) _____ book.
7. John reads (sus, *de él*) _____ letters.
8. I eat (mi) _____ candy.
9. Father likes (su, *de él*) _____ old car.
10. John and Robert go with (su, *de ellos*) _____ mother.

EXERCISE 6
Práctica verbal. *Amplíe las siguientes formas hasta incluir todas las personas.*

1. I live in Mexico.
2. I like to live in Mexico.
3. I can live in Mexico.
4. I can't live in Mexico.
5. Can I live in Mexico?
6. Can't I live in Mexico?

EXERCISE 7
Práctica verbal. *Repita el ejercicio 6, usando formas de los verbos* **eat** *(apples),* **bring** *(candy),* **read** *(English),* **help** *(John),* **write** *(letters),* **say** *(good morning),* **use** *(a phone),* **go** *(to the movies).*

LESSON 5

EXERCISE 8
Lea y traduzca estas oraciones.

1. Her brother likes to live in the United States.
2. Some of the boys go to the park.
3. There are many nice houses in that city.
4. All the girls take their books to school.
5. Our last name is Miller.
6. How many pencils can you bring?
7. Our sisters help our mother in the house.
8. The girls eat dinner with their brothers.
9. We can' t take that book. It's very big.
10. There's no room in this car.
11. Her first name is Margaret. Her last name is Wells.
12. He likes to go to the office with his father.
13. one, two, three, four, five, six, seven, eight, nine, ten.
14. 6, 2, 3, 4, 10, 7, 9, 5, 8, 7, 2, 5, 10, 4.

EXERCISE 9
Escriba en inglés.

1. No hay lugar en su (*de ellos*) casa.
2. Hay un parque en esta ciudad. Es muy grande.
3. A mis hermanos y a mí nos gustan los dulces.
4. Me llamo Pedro. Mi apellido es Daniels.
5. Él lleva a todos sus pequeños hermanos a la ciudad.
6. ¿Dónde está el teléfono? Aquí está.
7. ¿Puede usted venir a mi casa con Alicia?
8. A ellos les gusta todo en esa ciudad.
9. No podemos leer este libro. Podemos leer aquél.
10. ¿No puedes escribir con este lápiz?

EXERCISE 10
Dictado

1. We like to go to the movies with our brothers.
2. They live in a nice house in Mexico City.
3. Our last name is Peterson.
4. Is there room in his house?
5. All those girls can take their notebooks to school.
6. Can you read all these letters?
7. Father likes to take the boys to school.
8. Her brother lives in that house.
9. My father likes everything.
10. We like to go to the movies with John.

EXERCISE 11
Conversación. *Conteste las siguientes preguntas en afirmativo y negativo.*

1. Is there room in the car?
2. Can you take your book to school?
3. Can you use this notebook?
4. Is John in the street?
5. Are your brothers in the United States?
6. Is Mexico City big?
7. Is that one little?
8. Are those cities small?
9. Aren't the boys here?
10. Can you read?
11. Can't Alice write?
12. Can Mary and Alice come to my house?
13. Can all the boys go?
14. Are all the boys in the house?
15. Is everything here?

Lesson 6

VOCABULARY

1. **to put** poner, meter
2. **to wash** lavar(se)
3. **to wait (for)** esperar
4. **to study** estudiar
5. **that** que
6. **but** pero, sino
7. **when** cuándo
8. **why** por qué
9. **because** porque
10. **now** ahora
11. **what** qué; lo que
12. **early** temprano
13. **late** tarde
14. **family** familia
15. **parents** padres
16. **child** niño, niña; hijo, hija
17. **children** niños, niñas; hijos, hijas
18. **garage** garaje; taller
19. **factory** fábrica

IDIOMS

1. Wait for me. Espéreme usted.
2. I like it. (*refiriéndose a una cosa*) Me gusta.
3. what time a qué hora
4. too + (adj. o adv.) = demasiado + (adj. o adv.)
   too big (late) demasiado grande (tarde)
5. too much (work) demasiado (trabajo)
   too many (books) demasiados (libros)
6. a lot mucho, muchos
   a lot of work mucho trabajo

44 LESSON 6

a lot of books muchos libros
(Se emplea **of** sólo cuando va seguido de un sustantivo.)
7. **very much** mucho
8. **What are you waiting for?** ¿Qué esperas?
9. **He's eating dinner.** Él está comiendo (*la comida principal.*)

EXERCISE 1
Traduzca las siguientes oraciones y practique leyéndolas.

1. He brings candy every day.
2. That man likes to bring books.
3. That man can bring Mary.
4. That man can't bring Mary.
5. We bring the children too.
6. Mr. Jackson and I bring a lot of apples.
7. Mr. Jackson and I like to bring a lot of apples.
8. Mr. Jackson and I can bring a lot of apples.
9. Mr. Jackson and I can't bring a lot of apples.
10. She eats very much.
11. That girl likes to read everything.
12. That girl can eat a lot.
13. That girl can't eat a lot.
14. They come late every day.
15. They like to come late every day.
16. They can come late every day.
17. The can't come late every day.

EXERCISE 2
Llene los espacios con **this, this one, these, that, that one, those** *y traduzca.*

1. When can (ese) _____ boy come early?
2. (Esta) _____ family waits for all the children.
3. (Esos) _____ parents wait for their children.
4. Why can't (esa) _____ girl work here?
5. John likes to wash (ese) _____ new car, and Henry likes to wash (éste) _____.
6. (Estos) _____ children like to go to school.
7. Where can I put (estas) _____ tables?

LESSON 6

8. Why can't you take (este) _____ child and (aquél) _____?
9. My father likes (esta) _____ house, but my mother likes (ésa) _____.
10. Mother says that (esa) _____ house is too little.

EXERCISE 3
Llene los espacios con la forma correcta del adjetivo posesivo y traduzca.

1. (Sus, *de ellos*) _____ children are very little.
2. Mr. Jackson washes (su, *de él*) _____ new car.
3. (Su, *de ella*) _____ brother waits for Mary in the street.
4. (Mi) _____ father puts the car in the garage.
5. (Nuestros) _____ children like to study English.
6. Can't (su, *de usted*) _____ child learn to write?
7. (Su, de él) _____ brother lives in the United States.
8. Mrs. Martin takes (sus, *de ella*) _____ children to the park every day.
9. "This is (mi) _____ pen," says Miss Jackson.
10. (Nuestro) _____ last name is Morgan.

La palabra home

home a casa	**from home** de casa
at home en casa	
He comes home every day.	Él viene a casa todos los días.
He goes home early.	Él va a casa temprano.
He's at home.	Él está en casa.
He works at home.	Él trabaja en casa.
He brings his books from home.	Él trae sus libros de casa.

EXERCISE 4
Traduzca al inglés.

1. Mi papá viene a casa.
2. Los niños van a casa temprano.
3. Venimos de casa.
4. Me gusta comer en casa.
5. Su papá (de ella) trabaja en casa.
6. Mis padres no pueden ir a casa.
7. ¿Está en casa tu hermano?
8. Ella puede traer muchos de casa.
9. ¿Puedo ir a casa?
10. ¿Por qué no puedes ir a casa?

El gerundio

El gerundio de los verbos se forma agregando **ing** al infinitivo, y suprimiendo la partícula **to**. **Going, working, reading, saying** son gerundios con la terminación **ing**. En castellano esta terminación corresponde a los sufijos **ando** y **iendo**.

going yendo	**reading** leyendo
working trabajando	**saying** diciendo

Si el infinitivo termina en **e** se suprime la **e** antes de agregar **ing**. Ejemplos: **come, coming; write, writing; use, using**. Excepciones: **being (siendo, estando); seeing** (viendo).

Los verbos monosílabos que terminan en una sola consonante, precedida de una sola vocal duplicarán la consonante final antes de agregar **ing**. Ejemplo: **put, putting**.

EXERCISE 5
Dé el gerundio de los siguientes verbos.

1. be
2. go
3. come
4. work
5. read
6. write
7. use
8. take
9. say
10. live
11. eat
12. help
13. bring
14. put
15. wash
16. wait (for)
17. study
18. learn

El tiempo presente progresivo

Las formas del presente del verbo **be** son **am**, **is**, **are**. El presente progresivo se forma con el presente del verbo **be** (que se usa en este caso como auxiliar) y el gerundio.

Este tiempo sirve para describir una acción que está ocurriendo en el momento actual. Compare las formas en inglés y en castellano.

Afirmativo

I'm studying.	Estoy estudiando.
He's working.	Él está trabajando.
You're reading.	Tú estás leyendo.

Negativo

I'm not working now.	No estoy trabajando ahora.
You aren't reading.	Tú no estás leyendo
She isn't working now.	Ella no está trabajando ahora.

Fíjese en el orden de las palabras del interrogativo. Al hacer preguntas en inglés, siempre se usa el auxilar antes del sustantivo o del pronombre. En el caso del presente progresivo se usarán como auxiliar las formas del verbo **be**.

Interrogativo

Auxiliar	Sustantivo o pronombre	Verbo
Are	they	writing?
¿Están	ellos	escribiendo?
(Why) are	the boys	writing?
¿(Por qué) están	los muchachos	escribiendo?

Interrogativo negativo

Auxiliar	Sustantivo o pronombre	Verbo
Isn't	he	studying?
¿No está	él	estudiando?
(Why) isn't	John	studying?
¿(Por qué) no está	Juan	estudiando?
Aren't	the girls	studying?
¿No están	las muchachas	estudiando?

EXERCISE 6
Traduzca las siguientes frases. Cámbielas al negativo interrogativo e interrogativo negativo.

1. I'm taking
2. you're living
3. he's putting
4. Robert is learning
5. she's studying
6. Mary is washing
7. we're working
8. they're reading
9. the boys are using
10. he's eating candy

EXERCISE 7
Práctica verbal

1. He's working now.
2. He isn't working now.
3. Is he working now?
4. Isn't he working now?
5. Where is he working?
6. Why is he working?
7. Why isn't he working?
8. At what time is he working?

EXERCISE 8

Práctica verbal. *Repita el ejercicio 7, usando formas de los verbos* **say** *(thank you),* **read** *(a letter),* **write** *(a book),* **use** *(the phone),* **take** *(his family),* **live** *(in the United States),* **eat** *(an apple),* **help** *(their father),* **bring** *(my notebook). Emplee un pronombre o sustantivo distinto con cada verbo. Use las palabras interrogativas* **what, where, when, why, why not, what time, how many** *cuando sea posible.*

EXERCISE 9

Llene los espacios con la forma correcta del verbo y traduzca.

1. (put)   My brother is _____ the car in the garage.
2. (work)   That girl is _____ in our house.
3. (wait for) We're _____ Mr. Smith.
4. (live)   Are you _____ in Mexico City?
5. (study)   What is Robert _____?
6. (study)   He's _____ English.
7. (learn)   Why are you _____ English?
8. (work)   Why aren't you _____ in the factory?
9. (go)   Why are all the boys _____ home?
10. (wash)   Why is John _____ the car?

EXERCISE 10
Práctica verbal

1. He waits for Mary every day.
2. He likes to wait for Mary.
3. He can wait for Peter.
4. He can't wait for Peter.
5. Can he wait for Peter?
6. Can't he wait for Peter?
7. When can he wait for Peter?
8. Where can he wait for Peter?
9. At what time can he wait for Peter?
10. Why can't he wait for Peter?
11. He's waiting for you.

12. He isn't waiting for you.
13. Is he waiting for you?
14. Isn't he waiting for you?
15. Where is he waiting for you?
16. Why is he waiting for you?
17. Why isn't he waiting for you?
18. What is he waiting for?

EXERCISE 11

Práctica verbal. *Repita el ejercicio 10, usando formas de los verbos* **study** *(a lot),* **learn** *(English),* **wash** *(the car),* **read** *(a book),* **put** *(the notebook here),* **go** *(home),* **come** *(home),* **eat** *(at home). Emplee un pronombre o sustantivo distinto con cada verbo. Use las palabras interrogativas* **what, where, when, why, why not, what time, how many** *cuando sea posible.*

EXERCISE 12

Lea estas oraciones y traduzca.

1. Bill is studying English, but he says he isn't learning very much.
2. Grace is studying English too, and she likes it a lot.
3. What are you waiting for? I'm waiting for my brother.
4. Mother says that she likes her house because it isn't too big.
5. John studies Spanish because he likes it.
6. The children wash the car, and John puts the car in the garage.
7. My parents go to work very early, and they come home very late.
8. What time can you wait for me?
9. Wait for me at home.
10. These children like to come home late.
11. Why can't you come to my house with your sister?
12. Mr. Miller can't work in the factory because he's very old.
13. What's your name? My first name is George and my last name is Parks.

EXERCISE 13
Escriba en inglés.

1. ¿Por qué estás trabajando en una fábrica?
2. Roberto está metiendo todo en el garaje.
3. ¿A dónde vas ahora? Voy a la escuela.
4. ¿Por qué no están ellos viviendo en Estados Unidos?
5. A Alicia le gusta estudiar inglés.
6. ¿Cuántos libros puedes leer? Puedo leer ése y aquél.
7. ¿Qué esperas? Estoy esperando a los niños.
8. A ellos les gusta mucho el inglés.
9. ¿Hay lugar en este coche y en aquél?
10. ¿Puedes ayudar a tus hermanos?
11. Él está comiendo muchos dulces.

EXERCISE 14
Dictado

1. My parents are going to the office, and I'm going to school.
2. These children like to read their books.
3. Are the children using the phone?
4. He can't write because there isn't a pencil.
5. Wait for me because I'm going with you.
6. What can I take with me to the park?
7. How many books are the children using?
8. Why are you using my pencil?
9. Why aren't the boys helping their parents?
10. What are you saying?

EXERCISE 15
Conversación. *Conteste las siguientes preguntas en afirmativo y negativo.*

1. Can you read?
2. Can John read?
3. Can you come early?

4. Can't they wash the car?
5. Can my brother wait for you?
6. Can all the boys go home?
7. Can't you learn everything?
8. Is that child Mexican?
9. Is that one American?
10. Are those children from this school?
11. Are these from that school?
12. Aren't you putting the car in the garage?
13. Is John coming?
14. Are you waiting for me?
15. Is that man waiting for you?
16. Are you working in a factory now?
17. Is he working in a factory?
18. Are you going to he factory?
19. Is the car too big?
20. Isn't the house too big?
21. Are there too many?
22. Are there too many cars?
23. Is there too much candy?
24. Are there too many children?
25. Is there too much room?

LESSON 6

Lesson 7

VOCABULARY

1. **to get up** levantarse
2. **to wake up** despertarse
3. **to visit** visitar
4. **to teach** enseñar
5. **to see** ver
6. **for** para, por
7. **so** así es que; para que; por lo tanto
8. **student** estudiante, alumno
9. **how much** cuánto
10. **who** quién
11. **please** por favor
12. **minute** minuto
13. **hour** hora
14. **husband** esposo
15. **wife** esposa
    wives esposas
16. **year** año
17. **tomorrow** mañana
18. **eleven** (11),
    twelve (12),
    thirteen (13),
    fourteen (14),
    fifteen (15)

IDIOMS

1. **They say.** Dicen.
2. **to be early** Llegar temprano.
   I'm early. Llego temprano; llegué temprano (*cuando uno acaba de llegar*).
3. **to be late** Llegar tarde.
   I'm late Llego tarde; estoy retrasado, he llegado tarde; se me está haciendo tarde; llegué tarde (*cuando uno acaba de llegar*).

4. **in the morning** En o por la mañana
5. **Just a minute please** Un momento, por favor
6. **It's very early.** Es muy temprano.
   It's very late. Es muy tarde.
7. **so + (adj. o adv.)** = tan + (adj. o adv.)
   so big (late) Tan grande, (tarde)
8. **so much (work)** Tanto (trabajo)
   so many (books) tantos (libros)

EXERCISE 1
Traduzca las siguientes oraciones y practique leyéndolas.

1. We put the car in the garage.
2. We like to put the car in the garage.
3. We can put the car in the garage.
4. We can't put the car in the garage.
5. Can we put the car in the garage?
6. Can't we put the car in the garage?.
7. They're washing everything.
8. They aren't washing everything.
9. Are they washing everything?
10. It's working now.
11. Is it working now?
12. Isn't it working now?
13. Why isn't it working?
14. There's too much room.
15. Is there too much room?
16. How much room is there?
17. There isn't too much room.

La preposición for

En inglés se emplea la preposición **for** para expresar duración de tiempo.

Muchas veces el equivalente de **for** en castellano no se usa porque la preposición queda sobreentendida en la oración.

> He studies **for** ten minutes.
> Él estudia diez minutos.
>
> I can work **for** two hours.
> Puedo trabajar dos horas.
>
> We can live in Acapulco **for** a year.
> Podemos vivir en Acapulco **por** un año.

EXERCISE 2
Llene los espacios con la preposición correcta y traduzca.

1. I can read _____ an hour.
2. All the students are studying (en) _____ school.
3. Are you waiting _____ your husband?
4. Some (de) _____ my brothers teach English.
5. Who lives (en) _____ 10 Grant Street?
6. There are two cars (en) _____ our garage.
7. How many notebooks are there (en) _____ the desk?
8. Who studies _____ fifteen minutes?
9. Charles works _____ two hours.
10. Can you go to the United States _____ a year?

EXERCISE 3
Llene los espacios con la forma correcta del verbo **be** y traduzca.

1. _____ you living in Mexico now?
2. The child _____ waking up.
3. George _____ working with his father.
4. Mrs. Brown _____ waiting for her husband.
5. We _____ putting everything in the house.
6. That man _____ teaching Spanish.
7. Why _____ you getting up so early?

8. Why _____ these girls studying?
9. Who _____ using the phone?
10. What _____ you eating?

EXERCISE 4

Traduzca las siguientes oraciones. Cámbielas al negativo, interrogativo e interrogativo negativo.

1. My husband is getting up.
2. Miss Taylor is teaching English.
3. The children are waking up.
4. Charles is visiting his brother.
5. We're learning English now.
6. That boy is using the phone.
7. The students are eating a lot.
8. That girl is washing.
9. I'm helping.
10. He's waiting for his brother.

El futuro idiomático

El futuro idiomático es una manera propia del inglés, que sirve para expresar tiempo en el futuro. El castellano también tiene un futuro idiomático, y la formación de los dos es muy parecida. Se necesitan tres cosas para formar este tiempo en inglés: el presente del verbo **be** (**am, is, are**), la palabra **going** y **un infinitivo**.

Compare el inglés con el castellano. Fíjese en el presente del verbo **be**, la palabra **going** y **un infinitivo** en ese orden.

Afirmativo

I'm going to work tomorrow.	Yo voy a trabajar mañana.
He's going to get up early.	Él va a levantarse temprano.
They're going to visit their parents.	Ellos van a visitar a sus padres.

Negativo

I'm not going to work.	No voy a trabajar.
He isn't going to get up early.	Él no va a levantarse temprano.
We aren't going to teach English.	No vamos a enseñar inglés.

Interrogativo

Fíjese en el orden de las palabras en el interrogativo. El auxiiar siempre va antes del sustantivo o del pronombre. En el futuro idiomático el auxiliar es siempre una forma del verbo **be**.

Auxiliar	Sustantivo o pronombre	Verbo
Is	he	going to get up?
¿Va	él	a levantarse?
Are	they	going to visit?
¿Van	ellos	a visitar?
(Where) am	I	going to work?
¿(Dónde) voy	(yo)	a trabajar?

Interrogativo negativo

Auxiliar	Sustantivo o pronombre	Verbo
Isn't	he	going to work?
¿No va	él	a trabajar?
Aren't	they	going to visit?
¿No van	ellos	a visitar?
¿(Why) aren't	they	going to teach?
¿(Por qué) no van	ellos	a enseñar?

EXERCISE 5

Traduzca las siguientes oraciones. Cámbielas al negativo, interrogativo e interrogativo negativo.

1. I'm going to work.
2. You're going to eat.
3. He's going to help.
4. She's going to study.
5. We're going to study.
6. You're going to teach.
7. They're going to wake up.
8. That boy is going to read.
9. This girl is going to go.
10. These children are going to come.

EXERCISE 6
Práctica verbal

1. We're going to take everything.
2. We aren't going to take everything.
3. Are we going to take everything?
4. Aren't we going to take everything?
5. Why aren't we going to take everything?
6. When are we going to take everything?
7. Where are we going to take everything?
8. What time are we going to take everything?
9. Why are we going to take everything?

EXERCISE 7

Práctica verbal. *Repita el ejercicio 6, usando las formas de los verbos* **see** *(my wife),* **be** *(at home),* **like** *(that house),* **wait** *(for Robert),* **come** *(home),* **bring** *(a lot),* **wash** *(the children). Use un pronombre o un sustantivo distinto con cada verbo. Emplee las palabras interrogativas* **why, why not, what, where, when, how many, how much, at what time** *cuando sea posible.*

LESSON 7

EXERCISE 8
Llene los espacios con el infinitivo entre parentesis y traduzca.

1. (to put) — My brother is going _____ the car in the garage.
2. (to work) — That girl is going _____ in our house.
3. (to wait for) — We're going _____ Mr. Smith.
4. (to live) — Are you going _____ in Mexico City?
5. (to study) — What's Robert going _____?
6. (to see) — He's going _____ the new house.
7. (to learn) — Why are you going _____ English?
8. (to work) — Why aren't you going _____ in the garage?
9. (to go) — Where are all the boys going _____?
10. (to be) — Why is John going _____ a teacher?

EXERCISE 9
Llene los espacios con el auxiliary correcto de las formas del verbo **be** *y traduzca.*

1. Charles _____ going to bring a lot.
2. That girl _____ going to wake up early.
3. We _____ going to visit Mr. Smith.
4. The teacher _____ going to get up.
5. _____ you going to teach in Mexico City?
6. What _____ Robert going to study?
7. They _____ going to see everything.
8. Why _____ you going to learn English?
9. Where _____ the boys going to go?
10. Why _____ Alice going to be a teacher?

EXERCISE 10
Práctica verbal

1. They get up early.
2. They like to get up early.
3. They can get up early.
4. They can't get up early.
5. Can they get up early.
6. Can't they get up early?
7. Why can't they get up early?
8. What time can they get up?
9. They're getting up now.
10. They aren't getting up now.
11. Are they getting up now?
12. Aren't they getting up now?
13. Why are they getting up now?
14. Why aren't they getting up now?
15. They're going to get up late.
16. They aren't going to get up late.
17. Are they going to get up late?
18. Aren't they going to get up late?
19. Why are they going to get up late?
20. Why aren't they going to get up late?

EXERCISE 11

Práctica verbal. *Repita el ejercicio 10, usando formas de los verbos* **teach** *(English),* **wake up** *(early),* **visit** *(their parents),* **work** *(in a factory),* **study** *(Spanish),* **see** *(the teachers). Emplee un pronombre o sustantivo distinto con cada verbo. Use las palabras interrogativas* **why, why not, what, where, when, what time, how many** *cuando sea posible.*

EXERCISE 12

Lea y traduzca estas oraciones y números.

1. They say that that young man is a very good English teacher.
2. I'm waiting for my wife, but she's late.
3. What time are you going to work in the morning?
4. They say that they aren't going to visit their parents tomorrow.

5. Just a minute please. I'm going to help you.
6. Charles is visiting his teacher who lives in the United States.
7. Why are you getting up so early?
8. I'm late this morning.
9. His sister eats a lot of candy.
10. Twelve, fifteen, ten, eleven, eight, fourteen, thirteen, seven, six, three, nine, five, two, one, four, eleven.

EXERCISE 13
Escriba en inglés.

1. ¿Qué vas a llevar? Voy a llevar todo.
2. Alicia dice que le gusta levantarse temprano.
3. Voy a ver quién está en casa.
4. ¿A qué hora vas a trabajar?
5. Estamos visitando a nuestros padres en Estados Unidos.
6. Me gustan todos estos (this) dulces.
7. ¿Cuántos profesores hay en la escuela?
8. ¿Viene un coche ahora?
9. Ella llega tarde porque se despierta tarde.
10. ¿Quién va a despertar a Bill en la mañana?

EXERCISE 14
Dictado

1. He says that he likes to teach English.
2. Is your brother going to be a teacher?
3. When are you going to learn English?
4. Why are you getting up so early?
5. Why are they going to come home so late?
6. Why are the children going to school so early?
7. There are fifteen boys and girls in that school.
8. I'm waiting for the teacher.

9. She can't come so early.
10. one, six, twelve, fifteen, eleven, seven, thirteen, three, eight, fourteen, four nine, five, ten, eleven, twelve.

EXERCISE 15
Conversación. *Conteste las siguientes preguntas.*

1. How many teachers are there in the school?
2. How many boys are there in the school?
3. How many girls are there in the school?
4. How many children are there in the street?
5. Where are you going?
6. Where is your brother going?
7. Where is your sister going?

Conteste las siguientes preguntas en afirmativo y en negativo.

8. Can you wait for me in the morning?
9. Are you early?
10. Are you going to get up early?
11. Isn't she going to be a teacher?
12. Aren't you visiting your brother in Mexico City?
13. Can't they come early in the morning?
14. Is Henry going to eat here?
15. Isn't he taking everything?
16. Is this one too big?
17. Is that one too small?
18. Are you going to wake up early in the morning?
19. Aren't we going to work tomorrow?
20. Can you see me now?
21. Is the school too little?
22. Are there too many phones?
23. Is there too much work?
24. Is there a lot of work?
25. Is there a lot?

Lesson 8

VOCABULARY

1. **to speak** hablar
2. **to walk** caminar, ir a pie
3. **to run** correr
4. **to feel** sentir (se)
5. **to want** querer
6. **by** por
7. **before** antes de (que)
8. **after** después de (que)
9. **sick** enfermo
10. **weak** débil
11. **happy** feliz, contento
12. **sad** triste
13. **there** allí, allá
14. **cousin** primo (a)
15. **grandmother** abuela
16. **grandfather** abuelo
17. **grandparents** abuelos
18. **garden** jardín
19. **yard** patio; espacio alrededor de una casa
20. **sixteen** (16), **seventeen** (17), **eighteen** (18), **nineteen** (19), **twenty** (20), **twenty-one** (21), **twenty-two** (22)

IDIOMS

1. **I'm sorry.** Lo siento; Siento que...
2. **Excuse me, Pardon me.** Con permiso, Discúlpeme.
3. **that's why** por eso
4. **surely, certainly** desde luego; con mucho gusto
5. **There's going to be work.** Va a haber trabajo.
6. **There are going to be children.** Va a haber niños.

EXERCISE 1
Traduzca las siguientes oraciones y practique leyéndolas.

1. John and Mary visit their cousin.
2. John and Mary like to visit their cousin.
3. John and Mary can visit their cousin.
4. John and Mary can't visit their cousin.
5. John and Mary are going to see that movie.
6. John and Mary aren't going to see that movie.
7. John and Mary are getting up.
8. John and Mary aren't getting up.
9. Are John and Mary getting up?
10. Aren't John and Mary getting up?
11. My grandparents are going to wake up.
12. My grandparents aren't going to wake up.
13. Are my grandparents going to wake up?
14. Aren't my grandparents going to wake up?
15. When are my grandparents going to wake up?
16. Why are my grandparents going to wake up?
17. What time are my grandparents going to wake up?
18. Mr. Jackson can teach everything.
19. Mr. Jackson can't teach well.
20. Can Mr. Jackson teach well?

Los días de la semana

Aprenda los días de la semana. Note usted que en inglés se escriben con mayúscula.

Monday	lunes	**Friday**	viernes
Tuesday	martes	**Saturday**	sábado
Wednesday	miércoles	**Sunday**	domingo
Thursday	jueves		

El uso de las preposiciones on, by

En general se usa la preposición **on** antes de los días de la semana.

> My father works on Sunday.
> Mi papá trabaja el domingo.
>
> Are you going to come on Tuesday?
> ¿Vas a venir el martes?

La preposición **by** se emplea en inglés después de verbos de movimiento con la idea de **pasar por** o **pasar frente a**.

> Can you come **by** my house this afternoon?
> ¿Puede usted **pasar por** mi casa esta tarde?
>
> She walks **by** my house when she goes to school.
> Ella **pasa frente** a mi casa cuando va a la escuela.

EXERCISE 2
Llene los espacios con la preposición correcta y traduzca.

1. We visit our grandparents _____ Monday, Wednesday, and Friday.
2. Mr. Johnson goes (frente a) _____ the school when he goes to work.
3. Father eats (antes de que) _____ he goes to the office.
4. I get up (después de que) _____ he goes to the office.

5. I go home (después de) _____ school.
6. They help their mother (antes de que) _____ they study.
7. We go to the park _____ Sunday.
8. John comes (por) _____ my house before he goes to school.
9. Can you come to see me _____ Monday?
10. Where are you going to be _____ Thursday?
11. He walks (frente a) _____ the office.
12. They like to walk (en) _____ the park every day.
13. Why are you walking (en) _____ the park?
14. Many (de) _____ the boys are going to come _____ Friday.
15. Is John going to visit his grandmother _____ Tuesday?

La forma posesiva

La forma posesiva de un sustantivo que se refiere a una persona o a un animal se construye agregando un apóstrofo ' y una **s**. Esta forma posesiva siempre va antes del sustantivo poseído. En el caso de los sustantivos que terminan en **s**, basta añadir el apóstrofo después de la **s**.

the boy's book	el libro del muchacho
the boys' books	los libros de los muchachos
the child's pencil	el lápiz del niño
the children's pencil	el lápiz de los niños
John's pen	la pluma de Juan
Charles' house	la casa de Carlos
Mr. White's car	el coche del señor White
his father's	el (los) de su padre (*de él*)

LESSON 8

EXERCISE 3
Traduzca las siguientes frases al inglés.

1. el libro de la muchacha
2. el libro de las muchachas
3. la mamá de los niños
4. la casa de la señora Martin
5. la esposa del señor Jackson
6. el hermano de María
7. el hermano de los muchachos
8. los hermanos de los muchachos
9. el coche de mi padre
10. el primo de Juan
11. la casa de la señora
12. la de tu hermano
13. los de mi profesor
14. la de Juan

EXERCISE 4
Llene los espacios con la forma posesiva del sustantivo indicado.

1. (grandfather)   We're going to my _____ house.
2. (cousin)   Your _____ car is in our garage.
3. (sister)   Where is her _____ husband?
4. (Mrs. Jackson)   Isn't _____ husband here?
5. (boys)   The _____ notebooks are on the desk.
6. (Charles)   Henry is going with _____ brother.
7. (Mr. Martin)   That woman is _____ wife.
8. (children)   How many of the _____ books can you bring?
9. (girls)   The _____ grandmother is sick.
10. (brother)   My _____ wife says that she feels weak.
11. (wife)   This is your _____ book.
12. (father)   Those are my _____.

El verbo want

La forma verbal que se usa después del verbo **want** es el infinitivo con la partícula **to**. Compare con el español. Estudie las siguientes oraciones:

> I want to go.
> Quiero ir.
>
> He wants to speak to John.
> Él quiere hablarle a Juan.
>
> They want to go.
> Ellos quieren ir.
>
> We want to visit our cousins.
> Queremos visitar a nuestros primos.

EXERCISE 5
Traduzca las siguientes oraciones y practique leyéndolas.

1. He wants to be a teacher.
2. You want to go to the movies.
3. He wants to work in a factory.
4. She wants to read that book.
5. We want to write some letters.
6. They want to use their English.
7. Robert wants to come early.
8. Stella wants to get up early.
9. The boys want to work in the yard.

EXERCISE 6
Práctica verbal

1. We speak English.
2. We like to speak English.
3. We want to speak English.
4. We can speak English.
5. We can't speak English.
6. Can we speak English?

7. Can't we speak English?
8. We're speaking English.
9. We aren't speaking English.
10. Are we speaking English?
11. Aren't we speaking English?
12. We're going to speak English.
13. We aren't going to speak English.
14. Are we going to speak English?
15. Aren't we going to speak English?

EXERCISE 7
Práctica verbal. *Repita el ejercicio 6, usando las formas de los verbos* **run** *(in the yard),* **walk** *(home),* **feel** *(sad). Emplee un pronombre o sustantivo distinto con cada verbo. Use las palabras interrogativas* **why, why not, what, where, when, how many, how much, what time** *cuando sea posible.*

EXERCISE 8
Lea y traduzca las siguientes oraciones y números.

1. I want to go to the office this morning and see his cousin's sister.
2. William says that after he works in the yard he likes to eat.
3. Are you going to visit your grandmother on Saturday before you go to the office?
4. Are you going by your brother's house when you go to work on Tuesday?
5. I feel weak after I work all morning.
6. The children's grandmother wants to bring a lot of apples.
7. Fifteen of the twenty boys in that school are studying Spanish.
8. The children can run in the yard, but the y can't run in the house.
9. Alice says that she likes to walk to school.
10. We aren't going to be late on Monday.
11. My grandfather's house isn't very big, but it's very nice.

12. Isn't your cousin living with your grandfather and grandmother now?
13. sixteen, nineteen, twenty, eighteen, seventeen, fourteen, fifteen, thirteen, six, four, three, seven, eleven, twelve.
14. one, two, three, four, five, six, seven, eight, nine, ten.

EXERCISE 9
Escriba en inglés.

1. Lo siento, pero no puedo hablar inglés.
2. Discúlpeme, por favor. Me siento mal.
3. Ella dice que su hermana habla mucho.
4. Mi abuela no puede correr. Por eso llega tarde.
5. Vamos a levantarnos temprano el miércoles porque vamos a la escuela.
6. Mi nombre no está en el libro de Juan. Está en el de María.
7. Voy a hablar inglés.
8. La niña de la señora Johnson está triste porque está enferma.
9. Los padres de mi esposo están muy contentos porque viven en la ciudad.
10. ¿Por qué corres ahora?
11. Quiero ser profesor.

EXERCISE 10
Dictado

1. I'm not going to speak English. I'm going to speak Spanish.
2. Henry's cousin is early, but his brother is late.
3. He wants to go to the movies with me.
4. I'm sick. I can't work.
5. John says that everything is new.
6. What's your brother's name?
7. That boy's name is Bill.

8. My grandparents are very old, but they're very happy.
9. Why aren't the children happy?
10. eight, five, eleven, thirteen, twelve, twenty, twenty-nine, nineteen, eighteen, twenty-six, twenty-three.

EXERCISE 11

Conversación. *Conteste las siguientes preguntas en afirmativo y negativo.*

1. Can you come on Monday?
2. Can your father come on Saturday?
3. Can you come by the house this afternoon?
4. Can I use John's notebook?
5. Is he using his brother's book?
6. Is he going to use his sister's pencil?
7. Is he going to walk to school?
8. Is the boy running?
9. Is his cousin going to the factory now?
10. Is he coming now?
11. Is John's book red?
12. Is this one your father's?
13. Isn't that one your brother's?
14. Are those Mary's?
15. Is there going to be a lot of work?
16. Is there going to be a lot?
17. Are there going to be a lot of children?
18. Are there going to be a lot?
19. Are the boys running too much?
20. Are you going to eat a lot of candy?
21. Are they going to want a lot?
22. Is she going to be a teacher?
23. Aren't the girls going to wake up?
24. Are we going to be late?
25. Are you going to be early?

Lesson 9

VOCABULARY

1. **to do** hacer
2. **to understand** entender, comprender
3. **to sit (down)** sentarse
4. **to know** saber, conocer
5. **to open** abrir
6. **around** alrededor de
7. **slow** despacio, lento
   slowly lentamente
8. **fast** rápido, aprisa
9. **wall** pared
10. **fence** cerca, barda
11. **door** puerta
12. **window** ventana
13. **living room** sala
14. **chair** silla
15. **sofa** sofá
16. **floor** piso
17. **rug** alfombra
18. **homework** tarea (*de escuela*)
19. **thirty** (30), **thirty-one** (31), **thirty-two** (32), **forty** (40), **fifty** (50), **sixty** (60), **seventy** (70)

IDIOMS

1. **Please sit down.** Por favor, siéntese.
2. **He's sitting (down).** Él está sentado.
3. **What time is it?** ¿Qué hora es?
4. **It's five (o'clock).** Son las cinco (*en punto*).
5. **It's five-thirty.** Son las cinco y media.
6. **It's five-fifteen.** Son las cinco y cuarto.
7. **It 's a quarter after five.** Son las cinco y cuarto.
8. **It's twenty (minutes) to five.** Faltan veinte para las cinco.
9. **It's a quarter to five.** Falta un cuarto para las cinco.
10. **It's ten (minutes) after five.** Son las cinco y diez.
11. **At five (o'clock).** A las cinco (*en punto*).

LESSON 9

EXERCISE 1
Traduzca las siguientes oraciones y practique leyéndolas.

1. Mrs. Carter wants to get up.
2. Mrs. Carter is going to want to get up.
3. Mrs. Carter isn't going to want to get up.
4. Is Mrs. Carter going to want to get up?
5. Isn't Mrs. Carter going to want to get up?
6. What time is Mrs. Carter going to want to get up?
7. Miss Bell wants to speak Spanish.
8. Miss Bell likes to speak Spanish.
9. Miss Bell is speaking Spanish.
10. Miss Bell isn't speaking Spanish.
11. Is Miss Bell speaking Spanish?
12. Isn't Miss Bell speaking Spanish?
13. Why isn't Miss Bell speaking Spanish?
14. Mr. Curtis runs fast.
15. Mr. Curtis likes to run fast.
16. Mr. Curtis can run fast.
17. Can Mr. Curtis run fast?
18. Can't Mr. Curtis run fast?
19. Why can't Mr. Curtis run fast?
20. When can Mr. Curtis run fast?

El presente del verbo do

Las formas del verbo **do** significan hacer cuando se usa como verbo principal. En el presente de este verbo la forma **do** se usa para todas las personas menos para la tercera persona del singular, pues para ésta se usa **does**. Ejemplos:

| I do the work. | He does the work. |
| Yo hago el trabajo. | Él hace el trabajo. |

Los auxiliares do, does

Do y **does** se usan como auxiliares en preguntas y negaciones con todos los verbos menos con las formas del verbo **be** y otros auxiliares como **can**. En el tiempo presente la forma **do** se emplea para todas las personas menos para la tercera persona del singular, pues para ésta se utiliza **does**. Cuando se usa el auxiliar **does**, el verbo principal no lleva **s** como terminación de la tercera persona del singular en presente, porque después de un auxiliar en inglés se usa el infinitivo sin la partícula **to**.

La contracción negativa de **do not** es la palabra **don't**, y la contracción negativa de **does not** es la palabra **doesn't**.

Afirmativo

I want	yo quiero
you want	tú quieres
you want	usted quiere
he wants	él quiere
she wants	ella quiere
it wants	ello quiere
we want	nosotros queremos
you want	ustedes quieren
they want	ellos quieren
they want	ellas quieren

Negativo

I don't want	yo no quiero
you don't want	tú no quieres
you don't want	usted no quiere
he doesn't want	él no quiere
she doesn't want	ella no quiere
it doesn't want	ello no quiere
we don't want	nosotros no queremos
you don't want	ustedes no quieren
they don't want	ellos no quieren
they don't want	ellas no quieren

Interrogativo
Recuerde el orden de las palabras del interrogativo: auxiliar, sustantivo o pronombre, verbo.

do I want?	¿quiero yo?
do you want?	¿quieres tú?
do you want?	¿quiere usted?
does he want?	¿quiere él?
does she want?	¿quiere ella?
does it want?	¿quiere ello?
do we want?	¿queremos nosotros?
do you want?	¿quieren ustedes?
do they want?	¿quieren ellos?
do they want?	¿quieren ellas?

Interrogativo negativo

don't I want?	¿no quiero yo?
don't you want?	¿no quieres tú?
don't you want?	¿no quiere usted?
doesn't he want?	¿no quiere él?
doesn't she want?	¿no quiere ella?
doesn't it want?	¿no quiere ello?
don't we want?	¿no queremos nosostros?
don't you want?	¿no quieren ustedes?
don't they want?	¿no quieren ellos?
don't they want?	¿no quieren ellas?

EXERCISE 2
Práctica verbal

1. He lives here.
2. He doesn't live here
3. Does he live here?
4. Doesn't he live here?
5. Where does he live?
6. Why does he live here?
7. Why doesn't he live here?

EXERCISE 3

Práctica verbal. *Repita el ejercicio 2, usando formas de los verbos* **say** *(good afternoon),* **take** *(his books),* **bring** *(her cousin),* **study** *(a lot),* **go** *(every day),* **work** *(fast),* **get up** *(late),* **speak** *(English),* **walk** *(home). Emplee un pronombre o sustantivo distinto con cada verbo. Use las palabras interrogativas* **what, where, when, how many, how much, why, why not, what time** *cuando sea posible.*

EXERCISE 4

Llene los espacios con **do** *y* **does** *y traduzca.*

1. I _____ speak a lot of Spanish. (*negativo*)
2. _____ you speak English? (*interrogativo*)
3. _____ he speak English? (*interrogativo negativo*)
4. _____ your brother get up early? (*interrogativo*)
5. That girl _____ study. (*negativo*)
6. Mrs. Carter _____ like to teach. (*negativo*)
7. _____ we like to run in the garden? (*interrogativo*)
8. They _____ want to go. (*negativo*)
9. My sister _____ want to run. (*negativo*)
10. _____ John like to walk? (*interrogativo negativo*)

EXERCISE 5

Traduzca estas oraciones. Cámbielas al negativo, interrogativo e interrogativo negativo.

1. You know that man.
2. He works here.
3. I open the door.
4. She sits in a chair.
5. We understand a lot of English.
6. You speak Spanish.
7. John lives in Mexico.
8. They read the book.
9. Mrs. Carter uses a pencil.
10. That boy goes to school.

El imperativo

La forma imperativa de la segunda persona del singular **you** (tú, usted) y de la segunda persona del plural **you** (ustedes) se construye con el infinitivo, sin la partícula **to**. No se expresa ningún pronombre. Para el negativo se coloca el auxiliar **don't** antes del infinitivo sin la partícula **to**. Estudie lo siguiente:

Run.	Corre.	Corra.	Corran.
Don't run.	No corras.	No corra.	No corran.
Go.	Vete.	Vaya.	Vayan.
Don't go.	No (te) vayas.	No (se) vaya.	No (se) vayan.
Eat.	Come.	Coma.	Coman.
Don't eat.	No comas.	No coma.	No coman.

EXERCISE 6
Práctica verbal

1. Come here. (*Ven.*)
2. Don't come here. (*No vengas.*)
3. Come here. (*Venga.*)
4. Don't come here. (*No venga.*)
5. Come here. (*Vengan.*)
6. Don't come here. (*No vengan.*)

EXERCISE 7
Práctica verbal. *Repita el ejercicio 6, usando formas de los verbos* **help** *(John),* **wait** *(for me),* **speak** *(fast),* **bring** *(the car),* **work** *(every doy),* **get up** *(early),* **read** *(that book),* **use** *(his telephone).*

EXERCISE 8
Práctica verbal

1. He does the homework.
2. He doesn't do the homework.
3. Does he do the homework?
4. Doesn't he do the homework?
5. He likes to do the homework.
6. He doesn't like to do the homework.
7. Does he like to do the homework?
8. Doesn't he like to do the homework?
9. He's doing the homework.
10. He isn't doing the homework.
11. Is he doing the homework?
12. Isn't he doing the homework?
13. He's going to do the homework.
14. He isn't going to do the homework.
15. Is he going to do the homework?
16. Isn't he going to do the homework?
17. He can do the homework.
18. He can't do the homework.
19. Can he do the homework?
20. Can't he do the homework?
21. Do the homework.
22. Don't do the homework.

EXERCISE 9

Práctica verbal. *Repita el ejercicio 8, usando formas de los verbos* **sit** *(here),* **open** *(the window),* **know** *(everything),* **understand** *(Spanish). Use un pronombre o un sustantivo distinto con cada verbo.*

EXERCISE 10
Lea y traduzca estas oraciones y números.

1. She doesn't like to sit in that big chair in the living room.
2. There's a fence around our yard.
3. He's sitting on the sofa with Helen.
4. When I open that window, I can see all the children in the yard.
5. Charles is late because he doesn't like to get up early in the morning.
6. Are they going to put the green rug on the living room floor?
7. I don't know why there are twenty-one doors in this house.
8. Where are you going at six-thirty?
9. Please don't speak so fast.
10. The sofa is too big for the living room.
11. My cousin says that he's going to come at ten-thirty.
12. twenty-five, thirty-five, forty-five, fifty-five, sixty-five, seventy-five, twenty-two, thirty-three, forty-four, sixty-six, seventy-seven

EXERCISE 11
Escriba en inglés.

1. No me gusta esta película.
2. Puedo ver a todos los niños en el patio.
3. ¿Qué hora es? Son las dos y media.
4. Va a venir a las siete y veinticinco.
5. ¿Por qué no viene él temprano? Faltan diez minutos para las nueve.
6. La pluma de esta muchacha no escribe bien.
7. No te sientes en el piso. Siéntate en el sofá.
8. No corras tan rápido. No vamos a llegar tarde.

9. La señorita Harris no quiere lavar las puertas y las ventanas esta mañana.
10. ¿Qué haces ahora? Hago mi tarea.

EXERCISE 12
Dictado

1. What time is it?
2. It's three-fifteen.
3. It's twenty minutes to eight.
4. Do you speak English?
5. No, I don't speak English, but I speak Spanish.
6. Do you want to walk around the garden?
7. Please sit down on the sofa. I want to put the books in this chair.
8. I'm going to open the door.
9. How many windows and doors are there in the living room?
10. twenty-seven, thirty-one, forty-nine, fifty-two, sixty-three, seventy-six, twenty-eight, thirty-four, forty-seven, fifty-one

EXERCISE 13
Conversación. *Conteste las siguientes preguntas.*

1. What time is it?
2. Where do you live?
3. Where does your brother live?
4. Where does your father work?
5. What time do you go to the factory?
6. What time are you going to the factory?
7. What time do you go home?
8. What time are you going home?
9. What are they eating?
10. What's he going to bring?

Conteste las siguientes preguntas en afirmativo y en negativo.

11. Is it ten-fifteen?
12. Do you live in Mexico City?
13. Do you work in a factory?
14. Does your wife work in a factory?
15. Does your husband work a lot?
16. Do you work in an office?
17. Does your sister speak a lot of English?
18. Do you know that man's name?
19. Do you know everything?
20. Do you like to study English?
21. Do you get up early?
22. Do you wake up at seven o'clock?
23. Do you want to wait for me?
24. Isn't there going to be a movie?
25. Aren't there going to be girls?

VOCABULARY

1. **to have** tener, haber
2. **to call** llamar
3. **to tell** decir, contar
4. **to think** pensar, creer
5. **to make** hacer (*con las manos*)
6. **if** si (*condicional*)
7. **near** cerca (de)
8. **clean** limpio
9. **dirty** sucio
10. **white** blanco
11. **blue** azul
12. **son** hijo
13. **daughter** hija
14. **curtain** cortina
15. **day** día
16. **week** semana
17. **month** mes
18. **eighty** (80), **eighty-one** (81), **eighty-two** (82), **ninety** (90), **one hundred** (100), **two hundred** (200), **three hundred and fifty** (350), **three hundred and fifty-one** (351), **three hundred and fifty-two** (352)

IDIOMS

1. **How old are you?** ¿Cuántos años tiene?
2. **I'm twenty (years old).** Tengo veinte (años).
3. **I'm (very) hungry.** Tengo (mucha) hambre.
4. **I'm (very) thirsty.** Tengo (mucha) sed.
5. **I'm (very) cold.** Tengo (mucho) frío.
6. **I'm (very) warm (hot).** Tengo (mucho) calor.
7. **I'm (very) sleepy.** Tengo (mucho) sueño.

8. **I'm (very) afraid.** Tengo (mucho) miedo.
9. **It's (very) cold.** Hace (mucho) frío, Está haciendo (mucho) frío.

    It's (very) warm (hot). Hace (mucho) calor, Está haciendo (mucho) calor.
10. **I'm going to be twenty (years old).** Voy a cumplir veinte (años).
11. **I'm going to be hungry, thirsty, etc.** Voy a tener hambre, sed, etc.
12. **It's going to be cold, warm.** Va a hacer frío, calor.

EXERCISE 1
Traduzca las siguientes oraciones y practique leyéndolas.

1. John's cousin understands English.
2. John's cousin doesn't understand English.
3. Does John's cousin understand English?
4. How much English does John's cousin understand?
5. Doesn't John's cousin understand English?
6. Mary's father likes to sit here.
7. Mary's father doesn't like to sit here.
8. Does Mary's father like to sit here?
9. Why does Mary's father like to sit here?
10. Doesn't Mary's father like to sit here?
11. Why doesn't Mary's father like to sit here?
12. This boy's sister knows a lot.
13. This boy's sister doesn't know a lot.
14. Does this boy's sister know a lot?
15. Doesn't this boy's sister know a lot?
16. That man's wife likes to do this.
17. That man's wife doesn't like to do this.
18. When does that man's wife like to do this?
19. Doesn't that man's wife like to do this?

20. Henry's cousin is going to sit down.
21. Is Henry's cousin going to sit down?
22. Isn't Henry's cousin going to sit down?
23. John's brother is opening the door.

La preposición at con tiempo y lugar

La preposición **at** se usa para indicar tiempo definido y lugar determinado. Ejemplos:

> I eat at two o'clock. I live at 269 Madison Street.
> Yo como a las dos en punto. Vivo en la calle de Madison 269.

EXERCISE 2
Llene los espacios con la preposición correcta y traduzca.

1. We go to school (a las) _____ six-fifteen.
2. The sofa is (cerca de) _____ the window.
3. Do you like to sit (en) _____ the sofa?
4. He's sitting (a) _____ the table.
5. I'm going to sit (en) _____ this chair.
6. The children like to sit (en) _____ the floor.
7. I get up (a las) _____ seven o'clock in the morning.
8. Are you going (a las) _____ seven-twenty?
9. Mr. Carter goes to the office (a las) _____ nine-thirty.
10. There are five students (alrededor de) _____ the teacher's desk.
11. The garden is (cerca de) _____ the house.
12. I go (frente a) _____ your house when I go to school.

To do, to make

Se traducen los infinitivos **to do** y **to make** por hacer, pero hay una diferencia en el uso de los dos.

En general **make** se emplea para expresar una acción manual, mientras **do** se utiliza para expresar una acción mental o en oraciones donde no se define el tipo de acción. Estudie los ejemplos.

1. She's making curtains. *(acción manual)*
2. He does the homework. *(acción mental)*
3. What are you doing? *(tipo de acción no indicada)*
4. I want two boys to do this work. *(tipo de acción no indicada)*

EXERCISE 3
Llene los espacios con la forma correcta de los verbos **do** *y* **make** *y traduzca.*

1. What do you _____ on Sundays?
2. My father is going to _____ a chair.
3. The girls want to _____ some candy this afternoon.
4. What's John _____ in the street?
5. The students are _____ their homework.
6. My mother is _____ a rug.
7. His cousin _____ all the work.
8. When are you going to _____ your English lesson?
9. They _____ cars in that factory.
10. How much work can you _____ in a day?

El verbo have (tener y haber)

I have	yo tengo	**it has**	ello tiene
you have	tú tienes	**we have**	nosostros tenemos
you have	usted tiene	**you have**	ustedes tienen
he has	él tiene	**they have**	ellos tienen
she has	ella tiene	**they have**	ellas tienen

EXERCISE 4

Traduzca las siguientes oraciones y practique leyéndolas.

1. I have a son.
2. I don't have a son.
3. Do I have a son?
4. Don't I have a son?
5. What do I have?
6. You have a daughter.
7. You don't have a daughter.
8. Do you have a daughter?
9. Don't you have a daughter?
10. He has two sisters.
11. He doesn't have two sisters.
12. Does he have two sisters?
13. Doesn't he have two sisters?
14. It has a big yard.
15. It doesn't have a big yard.
16. Does it have a big yard?
17. Doesn't it have a big yard?
18. Why does it have a big yard?
19. We have our notebooks.
20. We don't have our notebooks.
21. Do we have our notebooks?
22. Don't we have our notebooks?
23. They have too much.
24. They don't have too much.
25. They're going to have too much.
26. Are they going to have too much?
27. Aren't they going to have too much?

EXERCISE 5

Llene los espacios con **have** *o* **has**.

1. We _____.
2. We don't _____.
3. He _____.
4. He doesn't _____.
5. John _____.
6. John and Mary _____.
7. John and Mary don't _____.
8. John doesn't _____.
9. They _____.
10. Don't we _____?
11. Doesn't Mary _____?

LESSON 10

EXERCISE 6
Traduzca estas oraciones. Cámbielas al negativo, interrogativo e interrogativo negativo.

1. John has two brothers.
2. Mr. Carter has two daughters.
3. We have a lot of candy.
4. My cousin has a phone.
5. George's brother has two books.
6. Mary and Bill have two pencils.
7. The windows have white curtains.
8. The children have parents.
9. Virginia has a lot.
10. The room has a red rug.
11. This car has everything.

La expresión idiomática de necesidad

La manera propia del inglés para expresar necesidad se forma con el verbo **have**, seguida de un ininitivo con la partícula **to**. Equivale a la expresión **tener que**, seguido de un **infinitivo**. Compare el inglés con el castellano.

Afirmativo

I have to go.	Tengo que ir.
He has to work.	Él tiene que trabajar.
They have to study.	Ellos tienen que estudiar.

Negativo

We don't have to read.	No tenemos que leer.
You don't have to wait.	No tienes que esperar.
I don't have to come.	No tengo que venir.

Interrogativo

Recuerde el orden de las palabras del interrogativo: auxiliar, sustantivo o pronombre, verbo.

Auxiliar	Sustantivo o pronombre	Verbo
Does	he	have to work? ¿Tiene él que trabajar?
Do	we	have to go? ¿Tenemos que ir?
Do	you	have to study? ¿Tienes que estudiar?

Interrogativo negativo

Auxiliar	Sustantivo o pronombre	Verbo
Doesn't	he	have to work? ¿No tiene él que trabajar?
Don't	we	have to go? ¿No tenemos que ir?
Don't	you	have to study? ¿No tienes que estudiar?

EXERCISE 7
Práctica verbal

1. He has to go.
2. He doesn't have to go.
3. Does he have to go?
4. Doesn't he have to go?
5. Where does he have to go?
6. When does he have to go?
7. Why does he have to go?
8. Why doesn't he have to go?
9. At what time does he have to go?

EXERCISE 8
Práctica verbal. *Repita el ejercicio 7, usando formas de los verbos* **work** *(late),* **speak** *(English),* **write** *(a letter),* **wake up** *(at eight),* **get up** *(at seven),* **be** *(early),* **have** *(a phone),* **live** *(in the United States),* **study** *(very much). Emplee un pronombre o sustantivo distinto con cada verbo. Use las palabras interrogativas* **what***,* **when***,* **where***,* **why***,* **why not***,* **how many***,* **how much***,* **what time** *cuando sea posible.*

EXERCISE 9
Traduzca estas oraciones. Cámbielas al negativo, interrogativo e interrogativo negativo.

1. Robert has to read his book.
2. All the children have to learn English.
3. We have to get up early.
4. You have to walk to the office.
5. Mary has to wait for me.
6. Mr. Carter has to wash the car.
7. The teacher has to teach English.
8. I have to use the phone.
9. We have to eat dinner.
10. That boy has to wake up.

La traducción de la partícula castellana a

La preposición **a** en castellano se usa entre el verbo y el complemento cuando el complemento es una persona o animal definido, pero no cuando se trata de un objeto.

Él lava a su hermanito.	He washes his little brother.
Él lava al perro.	He washes the dog.
Él lava el coche.	He washes the car.

En el último ejemplo la preposición **a** no se usa entre el verbo **lava** y el complemento **coche** porque **coche** no es ni persona ni animal. En inglés siempre se suprime esta preposición, cualquiera que sea el complemento: persona, animal u objeto.

EXERCISE 10
Traduzca las siguientes oraciones al inglés. No traduzca la preposición **a**.

1. Yo conozco a este muchacho.
2. Las muchachas no ayudan mucho a su mamá.
3. Juan visita a su abuela.
4. Él no enseña a los niños.
5. Yo puedo ver a mis padres.
6. Jorge está lavando el coche.
7. El maestro está ayudando a todos los niños.
8. Vamos a visitar a nuestros primos.
9. Yo no voy a despertar a aquellos muchachos.
10. ¿Por qué no vas a llamar a esos muchachos?

La traducción de for antes de un infinitivo

No se puede usar en inglés la palabra **for** (para) antes de un infinitivo como se usa en castellano.

Ejemplo: Es demasiado tarde **para** comer.
It's too late to eat.

EXERCISE 11

*Traduzca las siguientes oraciones al inglés. No traduzca la palabra **para** antes de un infinitivo.*

1. Él tiene todo para hacer la mesa.
2. Él usa su lápiz para escribir.
3. Él es muy pequeño para ir a la escuela.
4. Es demasiado temprano para levantarse.
5. ¿Qué tiene usted para comer?
6. Ella va a estudiar para ser maestra.
7. Hace demasiado calor para trabajar.

Reglas de ortografía

Cuando un verbo termina en **y**, precedido por una consonante, se cambia la **y** por **i** y se le agrega **es** para formar la tercera persona del singular. Ejemplo: **He studies**.

Los sustantivos terminados en **y**, precedidos por una consonante, forman su plural cambiando la **y** por **i** y agregando la terminación **es**. Ejemplos: **city**, **cities**; **country**, **countries**; **family**, **families**.

Recuerde la regla que aprendió en la lección 6. Para hacer el gerundio, cuando el verbo termina en **e**, se suprime ésta antes de agregar **ing**. Ejemplos: **give**, **giving**; **come**, **coming**.

Los verbos monosílabos que terminan en una sola consonante, precedida de una sola vocal, duplicarán la consonante final antes de agregar **ing**. Ejemplo: **put**, **putting**.

Esta regla se aplicará también a los verbos polisílabos cuando la última sílaba lleva el acento. Ejemplos: **begin** (empezar), **beginning** pero: **open**, **opening** (no se duplica la consonante, porque lleva el acento en la primera sílaba).

EXERCISE 12
Fíjese en las siguientes palabras.

1. cities
2. countries
3. families
4. studies
5. coming
6. writing
7. using
8. taking
9. living
10. liking
11. getting up
12. waking up
13. seeing
14. putting
15. running
16. sitting (down)

EXERCISE 13
Práctica verbal

1. She calls early.
2. She doesn't call early.
3. Does she call early?
4. Doesn't she call early?
5. Why does she call early?
6. When does she call early?
7. She's going to call early.
8. She isn't going to call early.
9. Is she going to call early?
10. Isn't she going to call early?
11. Why is she going to call early?
12. Why isn't she going to call early?
13. She's calling early.
14. She isn't calling early.
15. Is she calling early?
16. Isn't she calling early?
17. Why is she calling early?
18. Why isn't she calling early?
19. She likes to call early.
20. She doesn't like to call early.
21. Does she like to call early?
22. Doesn't she like to call early?
23. Why doesn't she like to call early?
24. She wants to call early.
25. She doesn't want to call early.
26. Does she want to call early?
27. Doesn't she want to call early?

28. Why doesn't she want to call early?
29. She can call early.
30. She can't call early.
31. Can she call early?
32. Can't she call early?
33. Why can't she call early?

EXERCISE 14

Práctica verbal. *Repita el ejercicio 13, usando formas de los verbos* **tell** *(John),* **think** *(that),* **make** *(curtains). Emplee un pronombre o un sustantivo distinto con cada verbo. Use las palabras interrogativas* **when, why, why not** *cuando sea posible.*

EXERCISE 15

Lea y traduzca las siguientes oraciones y números.

1. I have to wash the curtains because they're dirty.
2. There are blue and white curtains on the windows, and there's a green rug on the floor.
3. Mr. Carter's little daughter is going to the United States in a month to study English.
4. I'm going to sit near the window where it's warm.
5. I'm going to call the boys and see if they're running in the yard.
6. Miss Davis says that she has to make curtains for all the windows in her house.
7. Do you think that you can make a rug?
8. He says he's forty-five years old.
9. If you're hungry, why don't you eat?
10. The wall is very dirty, so don't sit near it.
11. Don't tell me that you're going to Chicago for a month.
12. Do you know how many months have thirty-one days?
13. fifty, sixty, seventy, eighty, ninety, one hundred, one hundred and ten, one hundred and twenty, two hundred
14. eighty-eight, ninety-nine, one hundred and twenty-two, one hundred and thirty-three, one hundred and fifty, one hundred and fifty-five, one hundred and seventy-five

EXERCISE 16
Escriba en inglés.

1. Abra usted las puertas y las ventanas.
2. No abras las cartas.
3. Si no puede usted venir el lunes, venga el martes.
4. Hace mucho calor en la sala. Por eso estoy abriendo las ventanas.
5. Mi hija tiene que estudiar inglés porque ella quiere trabajar en Estados Unidos.
6. Mi hijo tiene veintiún años, y por eso va a Estados Unidos para estudiar.
7. Llame a los niños. Creo que están en el patio.
8. ¿Cuántos niños tiene usted?
9. Ella está haciendo muchas cortinas para usar en su casa.
10. Tengo que trabajar el domingo.

EXERCISE 17
Dictado

1. Is it warm in Acapulco?
2. Yes, it's very warm there.
3. There are seven days in a week and thirty days in a month.
4. Some months have thirty-one days.
5. How many weeks are there in a month?
6. I have to go now. It's three-fifteen.
7. If you can't come on Friday, do you think you can come on Saturday?
8. He doesn't have to work on Tuesday.
9. If you're cold, don't sit near the window.
10. Why are you sleepy?

EXERCISE 18
Conversación. *Conteste las siguientes preguntas.*

1. How old are you?
2. How old is your brother?
3. How old is your sister?
4. How old is your car?
5. How many brothers do you have?
6. How many sisters do you have?
7. How old are you going to be?
8. What are you doing?
9. What are you making?
10. Does he have to work on Saturday?
11. Do you have to get up at six?
12. Do they have to study a lot?

Conteste las siguientes preguntas en afirmativo y en negativo.

13. Is she cold?
14. Is she going to be cold?
15. Are you sleepy?
16. Are you going to be sleepy?
17. Are they afraid?
18. Are they going to be afraid?
19. Is John's sister hungry?
20. Is John's sister going to be hungry?
21. Is it cold?
22. Is it going to be cold?
23. Is it hot?
24. Is it going to be hot?
25. Is there going to be homework?

VOCABULARY

1. **to think about** pensar en (*acerca de algo o alguien*)
   to think of pensar en (*algo o alguien*)
2. **to look (at)** mirar; fijarse (en)
3. **to clean** limpiar
4. **to talk** hablar; platicar
5. **to finish** acabar, terminar
6. **next** próximo, siguiente
7. **next to** junto a
8. **bad** malo, mal
9. **every** cada
10. **uncle** tío
11. **aunt** tía
12. **room** cuarto
13. **dining room** comedor
14. **vase** florero
15. **flower** flor
16. **money** dinero
17. **time** vez; tiempo
18. **first** (1st) primero
    second (2nd) segundo
    third (3rd) tercero
    fourth (4th) cuarto
    fifth (5th) quinto

IDIOMS

1. **I was ten (years old) in June.** Cumplí diez (años) en junio.
2. **over there** para allá, hacia allá, por allá
3. **over here** para acá, hacia acá, por acá
4. **every morning** todas las mañanas
   every afternoon todas las tardes
   every night todas las noches
5. **next week** la semana entrante; la semana próxima

next month el mes entrante; el mes próximo
next year el año entrante; el año próximo
6. **What's it made of?** ¿De qué es? ¿De qué está hecho?
   What's the door made of? ¿De qué es la puerta?
   It's made of wood, metal, glass, etc. Es de madera, metal, cristal, etc.
7. **I was hungry, thirsty, etc.** Tenía hambre, sed, etc.
8. **It was cold, warm.** Hacía (hizo) frío, calor.

El tiempo pasado del verbo be

El pasado de **am** y de **is** es **was**, y el pasado de **are** es **were**. La contracción en negativo de **was not** es la palabra **wasn't**, y la contracción en negativo de **were not** es la palabra **weren't**.

Afirmativo

I was yo estuve, estaba, fui, era	**it was** ello estuvo, fue
you were tú estuviste	**we were** nosotros estuvimos, éramos
you were usted estuvo, fue	**you were** Uds. estuvieron, eran
he was él estuvo, fue	**they were** ellos estuvieron, eran
she was ella estuvo, fue	**they were** ellas estuvieron, eran

Negativo

I wasn't yo no estuve, no estaba, no fui, no era	**we weren't** nosotros no estuvimos, fuimos
you weren't tú no estuviste	**you weren't** ustedes no estuvieron, fueron
you weren't usted no estuvo, fue	**they weren't** ellos no estuvieron, fueron
he wasn't él no estuvo, fue	**they weren't** ellas no estuvieron, fueron
she wasn't ella no estuvo, fue	
it wasn't ello no estuvo, fue	

Interrogativo

was I? ¿yo estuve, estaba, fui, era?	**was it?** ¿ello estuvo?
were you? ¿tú estuviste?	**were we?** ¿nosotros estuvimos?
were you? ¿usted estuvo?	**were you?** ¿ustedes estuvieron?
was he? ¿él estuvo?	**were they?** ¿ellos estuvieron?
was she? ¿ella estuvo?	**were they?** ¿ellas estuvieron?

Interrogativo negativo

wasn't I? ¿yo no estuve, no estaba, no fui, no era?	**wasn't it?** ¿ello no estuvo?
weren't you? ¿tú no estuviste?	**weren't we?** ¿nosotros no estuvimos?
weren't you? ¿usted no estuvo?	**weren't you?** ¿ustedes no estuvieron?
wasn't he? ¿él no estuvo?	**weren't they?** ¿ellos no estuvieron?
wasn't she? ¿ella no estuvo?	**weren't they?** ¿ellas no estuvieron?

EXERCISE 1
Traduzca las siguientes oraciones y practique leyéndolas.

1. I was sick.
2. I wasn't sick.
3. Was I sick?
4. Wasn't I sick?
5. You were sad.
6. You weren't sad.
7. Were you sad?
8. Weren't you sad?
9. He was dirty.
10. He wasn't dirty.
11. Was he dirty?
12. Wasn't he dirty?
13. She was clean.
14. She wasn't clean.
15. Was she clean?
16. Wasn't she clean?
17. We were happy.
18. We weren't happy.

19. Were we happy?
20. Weren't we happy?
21. You were weak.
22. You weren't weak.
23. Were you weak?
24. Weren't you weak?
25. They were late.
26. They weren't late.
27. Were they late?
28. Weren't they late?
29. It was dirty.
30. She wasn't early.
31. We were early.
32. It wasn't clean.
33. You weren't there.
34. Were they there?

EXERCISE 2
Práctica verbal. *Repita el ejercicio 1, usando sustantivos distintos.*

EXERCISE 3
Traduzca las siguientes oraciones. Cámbielas al negativo, interrogativo e interrogativo negativo.

1. I was here.
2. You were at home.
3. He was in the yard.
4. She was in the living room.
5. We were there.
6. You were on the sofa.
7. They were near the chair.
8. John was in the garden.
9. Mary was in the house.
10. John and Mary were there.

EXERCISE 4
Traduzca las siguientes oraciones y practique leyéndolas.

1. I'm hungry.
2. I'm not hungry.
3. Am I hungry?
4. Am I not hungry?
5. You're thirsty.
6. You aren't thirsty.
7. Are you thirsty?
8. Aren't you thirsty?
9. He's cold.
10. He isn't cold.

11. Is he cold?
12. Isn't he cold?
13. She's warm.
14. She isn't warm.
15. Is she warm?
16. Isn't she warm?
17. We're sleepy.
18. We aren't sleepy.
19. Are we sleepy?
20. Aren't we sleepy?
21. You're afraid.
22. You aren't afraid.
23. Are you afraid?
24. Aren't you afraid?
25. It's warm.
26. It isn't warm.
27. Is it warm?
28. Isn't it warm?
29. I was hungry.
30. I wasn't hungry.
31. Was I hungry?
32. Wasn't I hungry?
33. You were thirsty.
34. You weren't thirsty.
35. Were you thirsty?
36. Weren't you thirsty?
37. He was cold.
38. He wasn't cold.
39. Was he cold?
40. Wasn't he cold?
41. She was warm.
42. She wasn't warm.
43. Was she warm?
44. Wasn't she warm?
45. We were sleepy.
46. We weren't sleepy.
47. Were we sleepy?
48. Weren't we sleepy?
49. You were afraid.
50. You weren't afraid.
51. Were you afraid?
52. Weren't you afraid?
53. It was cold.
54. It wasn't cold.
55. Was it cold?
56. Wasn't it cold?

EXERCISE 5

Traduzca estas oraciones. Cámbielas al tiempo pasado y tradúzcalas.

1. It's time to eat.
2. What are the vases made of?
3. What's it made of?
4. It isn't cold.
5. He isn't sleepy.
6. We aren't afraid.
7. They aren't hungry.
8. My uncle is warm.
9. My aunt is thirsty.
10. My brother is hungry.

EXERCISE 6

Llene los espacios con la preposición correcta y traduzca.

1. The dining room is (junto a) _____ the living room.
2. There's a vase (en) _____ the dining room table.
3. There are a lot of flowers (en) _____ the vase.
4. Do you live (cerca de) _____ the school?
5. I think (en) _____ my family.
6. He looks _____ (a) the teacher.
7. We're going to Acapulco (por) _____ two weeks.
8. I can come (por) _____ his house at twelve-thirty.
9. Why are you waiting (a) _____ me?
10. There's a wall (alrededor de) _____ our house.
11. There aren't classes (en) _____ Sunday.
12. I was here (antes que) _____ you.
13. We think (en) _____ our children.

Los meses del año

Aprenda los nombres de los meses del año. Note que se escriben con letra mayúscula.

1. **January**	enero	4. **April**	abril
2. **February**	febrero	5. **May**	mayo
3. **March**	marzo	6. **June**	junio

Cuando no se indica el día exacto del mes, se usa la preposición **in** antes del nombre del mes. Ejemplos: **in January, in March, in June**.

Cuando se indica el día exacto, se usan las preposiciones **on** y **of** con el número ordinal. Ejemplos: **on the 5th of June, on the 1st of January, on the 2nd of March**.

EXERCISE 7
Llene los espacios con la preposición correcta y traduzca.

1. He was here _____ the 3rd _____ April.
2. I was in the United States _____ March.
3. Are you going to visit me _____ June?
4. Are you going to visit me _____ the 4th _____ January?
5. There aren't classes _____ the 5th _____ May.
6. Mr. Martin doesn't work _____ the 5th _____ February.
7. I'm going to Cuernavaca _____ April.
8. Were you here _____ June?
9. We can't go to school _____ the 1st _____ January.
10. Alice was with her mother _____ May.

EXERCISE 8
Práctica verbal

1. He thinks about his family.
2. He doesn't think about his family.
3. Does he think about his family?
4. Doesn't he think about his family?
5. When does he think about his family?
6. Why does he think about his family?
7. Why doesn't he think about his family?
8. He's thinking about his brother.
9. He isn't thinking about his brother.
10. Is he thinking about his brother?
11. Isn't he thinking about his brother?
12. Why is he thinking about his brother?
13. He's going to think about his mother.
14. He isn't going to think about his mother.
15. Is he going to think about his mother?
16. Isn't he going to think about his mother?
17. Why is he going to think about his mother?

18. When is he going to think about his mother?
19. He likes to think about that.
20. He doesn't like to think about that.
21. Does he like to think about that?
22. Doesn't he like to think about that?
23. Why does he like to think about that?
24. Why doesn't he like to think about that?
25. He can think about that next year.
26. He can't think about that next year.
27. Can he think about that next year?
28. Can't he think about that next year?
29. When can he think about that?
30. Why can't he think about that next year?
31. He has to think of his parents.
32. He doesn't have to think of his parents.
33. Does he have to think of his parents?
34. Doesn't he have to think of his parents?
35. Why does he have to think of his parents?

EXERCISE 9
Práctica verbal. *Repita el ejercicio 8, usando formas de los verbos* **look (at), clean, talk, finish** *en oraciones cortas. Emplee un sustantivo o pronombre distinto con cada verbo. Use las palabras interrogativas* **what, when, why, why not** *cuando sea posible.*

EXERCISE 10
Lea y traduzca estas oraciones y números.

1. I don't like to look at those flowers in that vase.
2. I have to clean all the chairs and the rug and wash the wall.
3. Sit down. I want to talk to you.
4. Frank's uncle lives on the third floor, and his cousin lives on the fifth.
5. Where were you this morning?
6. We have to eat on the second floor because the dining room is there.
7. It was very cold this morning.

8. The dining room table is made of wood, metal, and glass.
9. Who lives on the first floor?
10. The fourth boy is Mr. Jackson's son.
11. I don't have an English book, so I'm going to take one of these.
12. Mr. Jackson lives over there in that big house, but he works over here in this office.
13. Alice visits her aunt and uncle every night.
14. 1st, 2nd, 3rd, 4th, 5th, 2nd, 1st, 3rd, 5th, 1st, 2nd, 3rd.

EXERCISE 11
Escriba en inglés.

1. Los niños de la señora Hunt tenían mucha sed.
2. ¿Dónde estuviste a las seis y media?
3. ¿De qué son sus cortinas (*de usted*)?
4. ¿Tiene tiempo de ir conmigo?
5. ¿Dónde estaban todas las cosas?
6. Veo a la hija del señor Jackson todas las tardes.
7. Voy a ir a la Ciudad de México el martes.
8. Mi primo está sentado junto a mi tía.
9. Yo creo que podemos acabar dentro de una hora.
10. Juan cumplió veinte años el 5 de enero.

EXERCISE 12
Dictado

1. How old are you? I'm twenty-six.
2. Why do we have to finish so early?
3. I think of you every day.
4. John is going to eat in the dining room when he goes home.
5. What are you doing on the third floor?
6. What's it made of? It's made of wood.
7. Is it time to eat?

8. Why were you in the dining room?
9. Was it time to go to school?
10. Was Mary with John in the yard?

EXERCISE 13
Conversación. *Conteste las siguientes preguntas.*

1. Where were you this morning?
2. Where was your brother?
3. How old are you?
4. How much money do you have?
5. What time were you there?
6. What's it made of?
7. What were they made of?
8. What's the chair made of?
9. What's the vase made of?
10. What are the doors made of?

Conteste las siguientes preguntas en el afirmativo y en el negativo.

11. Were you late?
12. Were you early?
13. Was it time to go?
14. Was it time to eat?
15. Were you there?
16. Was John's cousin there?
17. Were the girls there?
18. Are you going to the United States next week?
19. Is John looking at the teacher?
20. Are you going to clean the living room?
21. Is he going to finish early?
22. Is she going to finish the work?
23. Are they talking to my mother?
24. Were you hungry?
25. Wasn't it very warm?

Lesson 12

VOCABULARY

1. **to ask** preguntar
   to ask about preguntar por, acerca de algo o alguien
2. **to answer** contestar
3. **to give** dar; regalar
4. **to turn on** encender
5. **to turn off** apagar
6. **last** último
7. **ready** listo
8. **then** entonces; después
9. **or** o
10. **picture** cuadro, pintura, película, fotografía
11. **kitchen** cocina
12. **stove** estufa
13. **radio** radio
14. **record player** tocadiscos
15. **light** luz
16. **water** agua
17. **gas** gas
18. **could** podía, pudo
19. **ninth** (9th) noveno
    twelfth (12th) duodécimo
    fifteenth (15th) décimoquinto
    twentieth (20th) vigésimo
    twenty-first (21st) vigésimo primero

IDIOMS

1. **Turn on the light.** Encienda la luz.
   Turn on the record player. Ponga el tocadiscos.
   Turn on the radio. Ponga el radio.
   Turn on the TV. Ponga la televisión.
   Turn on the water. Abra la llave del agua.

LESSON 12 107

2. **Turn off the light.** Apague la luz.
   Turn off the record player. Apague el tocadiscos.
   Turn off the radio. Apague el radio.
   Turn off the TV. Apague la televisión.
   Turn off the water. Cierre la llave del agua.
3. **to ask** pedirle (*a alguien*)
   Ask your mother. Pídele a tu mamá.
   to ask for pedir (*algo*)
   Ask for the book. Pide el libro.
   to ask someone for something pedirle a alguien algo
   Ask your mother for the book. Pídele el libro a tu mamá.
4. **Don't tell me.** No me diga.
5. **What were you doing?** ¿Qué estaba haciendo? ¿Qué hacía?
6. **I'm afraid to go, to come, etc.** Tengo miedo de ir, venir, etc.
7. **I'm afraid of John, of the water, etc.** Le tengo miedo a Juan, al agua, etc.
8. **on Friday morning** el viernes en la mañana
   on Monday afternoon el lunes en la tarde
   on Sunday night el domingo en la noche

EXERCISE 1
Traduzca las siguientes oraciones y practique leyéndolas.

1. Come early.
2. Don't come too early.
3. That man is looking at the house.
4. That man isn't looking at the house.
5. Is that man looking at the house?
6. Isn't that man looking at the house?
7. That girl is going to clean the windows.
8. That girl isn't going to clean the windows.
9. Is that girl going to clean the windows?
10. Isn't that girl going to clean the windows?
11. These boys like to speak English.
12. These boys don't like to speak English.

13. Do these boys like to speak English?
14. Don't these boys like to speak English?
15. Those children want to finish early.
16. Those children don't want to finish early.
17. Do those children want to finish early?
18. Don't those children want to finish early?
19. This man can speak Spanish.
20. This man can't speak Spanish.
21. Can this man speak Spanish?
22. Can't this man speak Spanish?
23. He was here very early.
24. He wasn't here very early.
25. Was he here very early?
26. Wasn't he here very early?
27. He's going to be hungry.
28. She's going to be sleepy.
29. They're going to be afraid.
30. You 're going to be hot.
31. I'm going to be thirsty.

El tiempo pasado progresivo

El pasado de la forma progresiva se construye con el tiempo pasado del verbo **be** (**was**, **were**) y el gerundio (la forma **ing**) del verbo empleado.

Este tiempo se usa para expresar una acción continua en el pasado o una acción que se llevaba a cabo mientras otra comenzó. Fíjese en los ejemplos.

> What were you doing? I was reading a book.
> ¿Qué hacías? Estaba leyendo un libro.
>
> I was washing the car when my father called me.
> Lavaba el coche cuando me llamó mi papá.

Afirmativo

I was working.	Yo estaba trabajando.
He was working.	Él estaba trabajando.
They were working.	Ellos estaban trabajando.

Negativo

I wasn't working.	Yo no estaba trabajando.
He wasn't working.	Él no estaba trabajando.
They weren't working.	Ellos no estaban trabajando.

Interrogativo

Recuerde el orden de las palabras para el interrogativo: auxiliar, sustantivo o pronombre, verbo.

Auxiliar	Sustantivo o pronombre	Verbo
Was	I	working?
¿Estaba	yo	trabajando?
Was	John	working?
¿Estaba	Juan	trabajando?

Interrogativo negativo

Auxiliar	Sustantivo o pronombre	Verbo
Wasn't	she	working?
¿No estaba	ella	trabajando?
Weren't	they	working?
¿No estaban	ellos	trabajando?

EXERCISE 2
Práctica verbal

1. He was cleaning the car.
2. He wasn't cleaning the car.
3. Was he cleaning the car?
4. Wasn't he cleaning the car?
5. When was he cleaning the car?
6. Why was he cleaning the car?
7. Why wasn't he cleaning the car?

EXERCISE 3
Práctica verbal. *Repita el ejercicio 2, usando formas de los verbos* **think about** *(of),* **look** *(at),* **finish, speak, make, open, call** *en oraciones cortas. Emplee un sustantivo o pronombre distinto con cada verbo. Use las palabras interrogativas cuando sea posible.*

EXERCISE 4
Traduzca las siguientes oraciones. Cámbielas al negativo, interrogativo e interrogativo negativo.

1. The boys were bringing the radio.
2. Helen's father was finishing his work.
3. Mrs. Jackson was making curtains.
4. George was feeling sick.
5. Robert's sisters were getting up.

El auxiliar could

Could es el pasado del auxiliar **can**. La contracción en negativo es la palabra **couldn't** que equivale a **could not**. La forma del verbo que se usa después del auxiliar **could** es el infinitivo sin la partícula **to**. Fíjese en los ejemplos.

Afirmativo

I could go.	Yo pude ir.
He could come.	Él pudo venir.
They could help.	Ellos pudieron ayudar.

Negativo

I couldn't go.	No pude ir.
He couldn't come.	Él no pudo venir.
They couldn't help.	Ellos no pudieron ayudar.

Recuerde el orden de las palabras para el interrogativo: auxiliar, sustantivo o pronombre, verbo.

Interrogativo

Auxiliar	Sustantivo o pronombre	Verbo
Could	I	go?
¿Pude	(yo)	ir?
Could	John	help?
¿Pudo	Juan	ayudar?
(When) could	they	help?
¿(Cuándo) pudieron	ellos	ayudar?

LESSON 12

Interrogativo negativo

Auxiliar	Sustantivo o pronombre	Verbo
Couldn't	I	go?
¿No pude	(yo)	ir?
Couldn't	John	help?
¿No pudo	Juan	ayudar?
(Why) couldn't	they	help?
¿(Por qué) no pudieron	ellos	ayudar?

EXERCISE 5
Práctica verbal

1. You could walk home.
2. You couldn't walk home.
3. Could you walk home?
4. Couldn't you walk home?
5. Why couldn't you walk home?

EXERCISE 6
Práctica verbal. *Repita el ejercicio 11, usando las formas de los verbos* **write, learn, bring, understand, go** *en oraciones cortas. Emplee un sustantivo o pronombre distinto con cada verbo. Use las palabras interrogativas cuando sea posible.*

EXERCISE 7
Traduzca las siguientes oraciones. Cámbielas al negativo, interrogativo e interrogativo negativo.

1. Those boys could read that book.
2. John's father could put the car in the garage.
3. That little girl could wait for her brother.

4. Mr. and Mrs. Jackson could take the children to the country.
5. John and you could teach Spanish.

EXERCISE 8
Traduzca las siguientes oraciones. Recuerde que en inglés no se usa la partícula **a** *entre el verbo y el complemento.*

1. Las muchachas estaban ayudando a su mamá.
2. Pregunte a su papá.
3. Llamen a los niños.
4. Voy a llevar a los niños al cine.

EXERCISE 9
Traduzca las siguientes oraciones. Recuerde que en inglés no se usa la preposición **para** *antes de un infinitivo.*

1. Vengo a la escuela para estudiar inglés.
2. Mis hermanos van a la casa de mi tía para trabajar.
3. El niño estaba estudiando para ser maestro.
4. No pudimos usar estos lápices para escribir.
5. Tenemos que encender la luz para leer.

Los meses del año

Aprenda los nombres de los meses del año. Note que se escriben con letra mayúscula.

1.	**July**	julio	4.	**October**	octubre
2.	**August**	agosto	5.	**November**	noviembre
3.	**September**	septiembre	6.	**December**	diciembre

EXERCISE 10
Llene los espacios con la preposición correcta y traduzca.
Acuérdese de la regla que estudió en la lección anterior.

1. It 's cold _____ December.
2. It 's warm _____ July.
3. We don't go to school _____ the 25th _____ December.
4. We don't have to work _____ the 20th _____ November.
5. What were you doing _____ October?
6. Were you here _____ the 10th _____ August?

EXERCISE 11
Práctica verbal

1. Ask the teacher.
2. Don't ask the teacher.
3. They ask their mother.
4. They don't ask their mother.
5. Do they ask their mother?
6. Don't they ask their mother?
7. Why do they ask their mother?
8. Why don't they ask their mother?
9. They're asking their father.
10. They aren't asking their father.
11. Are they asking their father?
12. Aren't they asking their father?
13. What are they asking their father?
14. Why are they asking their father?
15. They were asking their cousins.
16. They weren't asking their cousins.
17. Were they asking their cousins?
18. Weren't they asking their cousins?
19. Why were they asking their cousins?

20. They're going to ask for water.
21. They aren't going to ask for water.
22. Are they going to ask for water?
23. Aren't they going to ask for water?
24. They like to ask for candy.
25. They don't like to ask for candy.
26. They want to ask for candy.
27. They don't want to ask for candy.
28. They have to ask for the money.
29. Do they have to ask for the money?
30. Don't they have to ask for the money?

EXERCISE 12

Práctica verbal. *Repita el ejercicio 11, usando las formas de los verbos* **ask about, ask someone for something, answer, give, turn on, turn off**. *Emplee un sustantivo o pronombre distinto con cada verbo. Use las palabras interrogativas* **why** *y* **why not** *cuando sea posible.*

EXERCISE 13

Lea y traduzca estas oraciones y números.

1. Turn off the water in the kitchen because it's running on the floor.
2. We're going to read first. Then we're going to speak English.
3. I was waiting for you. Why were you late?
4. If you're ready to go, please turn off the light.
5. Please turn on the lights in the dining room because I want to eat. Then turn on the lights in the living room because I want to read.
6. Were you working at six-thirty this morning?
7. Don't tell me that you aren't going to give me the money.
8. What were you doing in the living room?
9. Why don't you ask your father or your mother if you can eat early?

10. Why couldn't he understand what you were saying?
11. We weren't hungry, but we were sleepy.
12. We're afraid it's going to be cold in the United States.
13. 1st, 2nd, 3rd, 4th, 5th, 6th, 7th, 8th, 9th, 10th, 15th, 16th, 17th, 18th, 19th, 20th, 21st, 22nd, 23rd, 24th, 25th, 31st 32nd, 33rd, 34th, 35th.
14. 18, 88, 17, 77, 16, 66, 15, 55, 14, 44, 13, 33, 19, 99, 20 200, 30, 300.

EXERCISE 14
Escriba en inglés.

1. ¿Qué estaban haciendo los niños en el patio todas las tardes?
2. ¿Tenías sueño el viernes en la noche?
3. No pongas la televisión porque estoy estudiando.
4. ¿Quién estaba escribiendo una carta en la sala?
5. Voy a venir el domingo 31 de agosto.
6. ¿Cuántos años cumpliste el diecinueve de agosto?
7. Aquella familia vive en el tercer piso. Ésta vive en el primero.
8. Él escribía una carta, y yo leía un libro.
9. ¿Por qué tenías miedo a esa mujer?
10. ¿Por qué no quieres venir para acá?
11. Ella va a pedir un radio a su mamá.

EXERCISE 15
Dictado

1. Those blue books are over there on that table.
2. He was seventeen years old on the 21st of January.
3. He's going to come on Sunday morning.
4. Why were you taking the radio to your room?
5. Why couldn't he live in Mexico City with his mother?
6. We couldn't go because we were late.
7. Do you like to answer the teacher in English?

8. That water in the kitchen is dirty.
9. Does Mary want to read in the living room?
10. Do you want to work in the kitchen?

EXERCISE 16
Conversación. *Conteste las siguientes preguntas.*

1. How old were you on the 4th of July?
2. How old is she going to be in June?
3. Where was your brother in September?
4. Why couldn't you go to school on Monday?
5. What's the stove made of?
6. What's the radio made of?
7. Where do you work?
8. What time is it?
9. What were you doing in my room?
10. Where was your brother on Tuesday?

Conteste las siguientes preguntas en el afirmativo y en el negativo.

11. Were you in New York in March?
12. Were you in Mexico City on the 5th of April?
13. Were you in the office at ten o'clock?
14. Were you turning on the record player?
15. Were you turning off the water?
16. Were you afraid of that man?
17. Were you afraid to sit in that chair?
18. Were you afraid to be in the garden?
19. Was he turning on the radio?
20. Could she ask the teacher?
21. Couldn't they ask for water?
22. Could she turn off the radio?
23. Couldn't they answer the teacher?
24. Is there going to be water?
25. Isn't there going to be light?

Lesson 13

VOCABULARY

1. **to look (for)** buscar
2. **to put on** ponerse
3. **to forget** olvidar
4. **to sleep** dormir
5. **to wear** usar (*ropa o joyería*), llevar puesto
6. **without** sin
7. **soon** pronto, rápido
8. **easy** fácil
9. **hard** duro; difícil
10. **today** hoy
11. **friend** amigo
12. **bedroom** recámara
13. **bed** cama
14. **shoes** zapatos
15. **hat** sombrero
16. **suit** traje
17. **dress** vestido
18. **there was, there were** había, hubo (*singular y plural*)
    was there? were there? ¿había? ¿hubo? (*singular y plural*)

IDIOMS

1. **When is your birthday?** ¿Cuándo es su cumpleaños?
2. **of course** por supuesto, claro (que)
3. **last week** la semana pasada
   last month el mes pasado
   last year el año pasado
   last night anoche
4. **tonight** esta noche
5. **I put on my hat.** Me pongo el sombrero.
   He puts on his suit. Él se pone el traje.
   (*En inglés se emplea el adjetivo posesivo con artículos de vestir.*)

LESSON 13

EXERCISE 1
Traduzca las siguientes oraciones y practique leyéndolas.

1. I'm afraid to go.
2. I'm not afraid to go.
3. They're afraid to come.
4. They aren't afraid to come.
5. He's afraid of John.
6. He isn't afraid of John.
7. Answer the teacher.
8. Don't answer the teacher.
9. Answer me.
10. Don't answer me.
11. Miss Monroe has to answer.
12. Miss Monroe doesn't have to answer.
13. Does Miss Monroe have to answer?
14. Doesn't Miss Monroe have to answer?
15. When does Miss Monroe have to answer?
16. Miss Monroe was asking for money.
17. Miss Monroe wasn't asking for money.
18. Was Miss Monroe asking for money?
19. Wasn't Miss Monroe asking for money?
20. When was Miss Monroe asking for money?
21. Why was Miss Monroe asking for money?
22. What was Miss Monroe asking for?

Había, hubo - there was, there were

There was y **there were** es el tiempo pasado de **there is** y **there are**. Equivalen estas formas a **hubo** o **había** en español. En inglés, a diferencia del castellano, **there was** se utiliza para el singular y **there were** para el plural. **Was there** y **were there** son las formas interrogativas, y **there wasn't** y **there weren't** son las formas negativas.

EXERCISE 2

Traduzca las siguientes oraciones. Cámbielas al tiempo pasado y traduzca.

1. There's a phone in the office.
2. There are four floors in that house.
3. There's a notebook on the desk.
4. How many beds are there in the bedroom?
5. How many of your friends are there in the living room?
6. There are thirty or forty children over there in the street.
7. Is there a chair in your bedroom?
8. Why is there a chair in the kitchen?
9. There are thirty-one days in December.
10. There are two cars in our garage.

EXERCISE 3

Traduzca las siguientes oraciones. Cámbielas al negativo, interrogativo e interrogativo negativo.

1. There were a lot of shoes in the bedroom.
2. There were two young American girls here.
3. There was a hat on the sofa.
4. There were two dresses next to the blue suit.
5. There was a man here this morning.
6. There were two cars in the street.

EJERCICIO 4

Traduzca las siguientes oraciones y practique leyéndolas.

1. There was a lot in the yard.
2. There were two boys in the park.
3. Were there too many boys?

4. Wasn't there a suit on the bed?
5. How many dresses were there in the bedroom?
6. Why weren't there five dresses?
7. There weren't two boys with Pete.
8. Were there two or three hats?
9. There was a man with my father.
10. There were two hats and a suit.

Adverbios de frecuencia

Aprenda estos adverbios de frecuencia.

1. **always** siempre
2. **usually** usualmente, generalmente
3. **often** a menudo
4. **seldom** rara vez
5. **rarely** rara vez
6. **sometimes** algunas veces, a veces
7. **ever** alguna vez, a veces
8. **never** nunca, jamás
9. **not... ever** nunca, jamás

Los adverbios de frecuencia se colocan antes de todos los verbos principales, menos con las formas del verbo **be**. Con las formas del verbo **be** se colocarán después, a menos que este verbo tenga otro auxiliar. El verbo principal es el verbo de la oración, que no es auxiliar.

El adverbio **ever** no debe emplearse en oraciones afirmativas; en estos casos, debe sustituirse por su equivalente **sometimes**, o algún otro adverbio, tal como **always**, **usually**, **often**.

Sin embargó, **ever** puede emplearse en oraciones interrogativas y cuando el verbo está en negativo.

Never equivale a **ever** con el verbo en negativo (**not... ever**). Estudie estas oraciones.

1. He can **never** come early.
   or
   He **can't ever** come early.

   (**never** y **ever** se colocan antes del verbo principal **come**)

2. He **never** comes early.
   or
   He **doesn't ever** come early.

   (**never** y **ever** se colocan antes del verbo principal **come**)

3. He's **never** early.
   or
   He **isn't ever** early.

   (**never** y **ever** se colocan después del verbo **is**, forma del verbo **be**)

4. Does he **ever** come early?
   or
   Does he **sometimes** come early?

   (**ever** y **sometimes** se colocan antes del verbo principal **come**)

5. Doesn't he **ever** come early?

   (**ever** se usa con verbo en negativo y se coloca antes del verbo principal **come**)

6. Does he **usually** come early?

   (**usually** se coloca antes del verbo principal **come**)

7. Doesn't he **always** come early?

   (**always** se coloca antes del verbo principal **come**)

8. Can't you **ever** be early?

   (**ever** se usa con verbo en negativo y se coloca antes del verbo principal **be** porque en este caso lleva auxiliar)

EXERCISE 5
Coloque los adverbios de frecuencia en su lugar correcto y traduzca.

1. (usually)   We work on Saturday.
2. (often)   They go to the movies on Sunday.
3. (sometimes)   John studies in the afternoon.
4. (always)   I am late.
5. (seldom)   The children speak English.
6. (rarely)   I visit my grandmother.
7. (never)   Mike eats a lot.
8. (always)   That child is sick.
9. (usually)   Those curtains are dirty.
10. (often)   Mr. Jackson is here.
11. (always)   He can't visit his friend.
12. (ever)   Is he here at eight o'clock?
13. (sometimes)   Are they here at eight o'clock?
14. (ever)   He doesn't get up early.
15. (usually)   Do they eat everything?
16. (always)   He can be here at six.

EXERCISE 6
Conteste las siguientes preguntas en el afirmativo y el negativo, usando uno de los adverbios de frecuencia.

1. Do you ever read that book?
2. Do you ever go to school on Saturday?
3. Do you ever visit your cousin?
4. Don't you ever eat mangos?
5. Don't you ever work on Sunday?
6. Don't you ever study your English?
7. Doesn't he ever write letters?
8. Does he always take his book?
9. Doesn't he always come early?
10. Do they often eat here?

11. Do they often write a lot of letters?
12. Don't they often see their parents?
13. Does she usually study on Monday?
14. Does she usually open the door?
15. Doesn't she usually study her English?
16. Does he sometimes go with you?
17. Does he sometimes answer in English?
18. Doesn't he sometimes speak Spanish?
19. Do you ever go to the movies?
20. Are you ever sleepy in the afternoon?
21. Do you ever see American movies?
22. Don't you ever wear a hat?
23. Is he always in the office at eight o'clock?
24. Is he always in the garden?
25. Isn't he always at the office in the morning?

El tiempo pasado del futuro idiomático

El tiempo pasado del futuro idiomático se forma con el tiempo pasado del verbo **be** (**was**, **were**), la palabra **going**, más un **infinitivo**. Compare el inglés con el español.

Afirmativo

I was going to work.	Yo iba a trabajar.
He was going to eat.	Él iba a comer.
They were going to come.	Ellos iban a venir.

Negativo

I wasn't going to work.	Yo no iba a trabajar.
He wasn't going to eat.	Él no iba a comer.
They weren't going to come.	Ellos no iban a venir.

Interrogativo

Recuerde el orden de las palabras para el interrogativo: auxiliar, sustantivo o pronombre, verbo.

Auxiliar	Sustantivo o pronombre	Verbo
Was	I	going to work?
¿Iba	yo	a trabajar?
Was	he	going to eat?
¿Iba	él	a comer?
(When) were	they	going to come?
¿(Cuándo) iban	ellos	a venir?

Interrogativo negativo

Wasn't	I	going to work?
¿No iba	yo	a trabajar?
Wasn't	he	going to eat?
¿No iba	él	a comer?
(Why) weren't	they	going to come?
¿(Por qué) no iban	ellos	a venir?

EXERCISE 7
Práctica verbal

1. They were going to be ready.
2. They weren't going to be ready.
3. Were they going to be ready?
4. Weren't they going to be ready?
5. When were they going to be ready?
6. Why weren't they going to be ready?

EXERCISE 8

Práctica verbal. *Repita el ejercicio 7, usando las formas de los verbos* **get up, wake up, finish, eat, make** *en oraciones cortas. Emplee un sustantivo o pronombre distinto con cada verbo. Use las palabras interrogativas cuando sea posible.*

EXERCISE 9

Traduzca las siguientes oraciones. Cámbielas al tiempo pasado y traduzca.

1. Henry is going to be a doctor.
2. Are you going to look at everything?
3. Aren't you going to look at my new dress?
4. She isn't going to turn off the radio.
5. My sister isn't going to speak English.
6. Are you going to sit in that chair?
7. When are they going to bring a lot of books?
8. Alice and Virginia are going to wash their dresses.
9. I'm not going to use my book on Tuesday afternoon.
10. My family isn't going to live in Mexico.

EXERCISE 10

Traduzca las siguientes oraciones. Cámbielas al negativo, interrogativo e interrogativo negativo.

1. We were going to study last night.
2. His friend was going to open all the doors.
3. She was going to learn the days of the week.
4. Our cousins were going to ask their parents.
5. Mike was going to put his hat in the living room.
6. They were going to visit Texas in October.

EXERCISE 11
Práctica verbal

1. He always looks for pictures.
2. He doesn't always look for pictures.
3. Does he always look for pictures?
4. Doesn't he always look for pictures?
5. Why does he always look for pictures?
6. He's always looking for pictures.
7. He isn't always looking for pictures.
8. Is he always looking for pictures?
9. Isn't he always looking for pictures?
10. He was always looking for pictures.
11. He wasn't always looking for pictures.
12. Was he always looking for pictures?
13. Wasn't he always looking for pictures?
14. Where was he always looking for pictures?
15. Why was he always looking for pictures?
16. He's going to look for the book.
17. He isn't going to look for the book.
18. He's never going to look for the book.
19. He isn't ever going to look for the book.
20. Is he ever going to look for the book?
21. Isn't he ever going to look for the book?
22. Isn't he going to look for the book?
23. He was going to look for his sister.
24. He wasn't going to look for his sister.
25. Was he going to look for his sister?
26. Wasn't he going to look for his sister?
27. Where was he going to look for his sister?
28. Why was he going to look for his sister?
29. He could look for the notebook.
30. He couldn't look for the notebook.
31. Could he look for the notebook?
32. Couldn't he look for the notebook?

33. Where could he look for the notebook?
34. He often likes to look for new friends.
35. He seldom likes to look for new friends.

EXERCISE 12
Práctica verbal. *Repita el ejercicio 11, usando formas de los verbos* **put on, forget, sleep, wear** *en oraciones cortas. Emplee un sustantivo o pronombre distinto con cada verbo y los adverbios de frecuencia cuando sea posible.*

EXERCISE 13
Lea y traduzca las siguientes oraciones. Lea los números.

1. I was going to go to the United States last month, but I couldn't because I was sick.
2. Henry thinks English is very hard to learn, but Ann thinks it's easy.
3. Is that my daughter or your daughter with the dirty dress?
4. That's your daughter. My daughter is over here.
5. This little girl is very sad because she has to wear her old dress.
6. The boys are very happy because they don't have to go to school on Friday afternoon; and, of course, the girls are happy too.
7. We were ready to eat, but we weren't hungry.
8. Why don't you put on your new suit and hat?
9. My friend can't go because he can't walk without his shoes.
10. Today is the last day of the month, and tomorrow is the first day of the new month.
11. They always eat in the dining room. They never eat in the kitchen.
12. Put on your blue suit. Don't put on your green suit because it isn't clean.

13. Where were you looking for your hat? It was in the bedroom.
14. 125, 250, 375, 400, 190, 280, 500, 366, 255, 144, 500, 422, 555, 666, 444, 333, 222, 111, 121, 21st, 22nd, 23rd, 24th, 25th, 26th, 31st, 32nd, 35th, 33rd, 41st, 42nd, 53rd, 54th, 71st, 62nd.

EXERCISE 14
Escriba en inglés.

1. ¿Por qué llevabas tu traje azul nuevo?
2. Había dos camas en la recámara.
3. ¿Qué buscas ahora? Busco mi cuaderno.
4. Por supuesto, voy a estudiar el lunes en la noche.
5. ¿Hubo un joven en aquel coche?
6. No se te olvide visitar a tu amigo pronto.
7. ¿Por qué nunca estudia él?
8. Rara vez aquella mujer visita a sus tíos (*tío y tía*).
9. Generalmente no uso sombrero.
10. Todos los niños iban a dormir en aquella cama grande.

EXERCISE 15
Dictado

1. Were you visiting your aunt and uncle in Mexico last year?
2. Don't forget to wear your hat because it's very hot.
3. My son puts on his shoes when he gets up.
4. I'm ready, so don't go without me.
5. It isn't easy to walk fast when you're wearing new shoes.
6. We're going to have flowers in our garden very soon.
7. I often go to my uncle's house, but I never see you there.
8. What are you looking for?

9. He says that he rarely gets up before ten o'clock on Sunday.
10. We couldn't go to the movies on Friday because it was very cold.

EXERCISE 16
Conversación. *Conteste las siguientes preguntas.*

1. What's the house made of?
2. What are the windows made of?
3. What's it made of?
4. How old were you in April?
5. When is your birthday?
6. Where do you live?
7. What time do you go to school?
8. What time do you go to work?
9. What are you doing?
10. What were you doing?
11. How many dresses were there in the bedroom?
12. How many chairs are there in the living room?

Conteste las siguientes preguntas en el afirmativo y en el negativo.

13. Do you ever like to get up early?
14. Do you ever like to get up late?
15. Does he sometimes want to visit his aunt?
16. Does he want to finish his work early?
17. Can they usually answer in English?
18. Do you ever go to the movies?
19. Was there a chair in the dining room?
20. Were there two record players in the house?
21. Are you going to sleep in the bedroom?
22. Were you going to sleep in the living room?
23. Is she cleaning the kitchen?
24. Was she cleaning the rug?
25. Can they turn on the water?

Lesson 14

VOCABULARY

1. **to go back, went back** regresar, regresó (*de acá para allá*)
2. **to laugh (at), laughed (at)** reírse (de), se rió (de)
3. **to pass, passed** pasar, pasó
4. **to fix, fixed** arreglar, arregló; componer, compuso
5. **to need, needed** necesitar, necesitó
6. **only** sólo, solamente; único
7. **each** cada
8. **yesterday** ayer
9. **bathroom** baño
10. **thing** cosa
11. **country** campo; país
12. **store** tienda
13. **question** pregunta
14. **lesson** lección
15. **word** palabra
16. **people** (*plural*) gente, pueblo (*población*)
17. **men** hombres
18. **women** mujeres

IDIOMS

1. **to ask a question** hacer una pregunta
2. **to watch TV** ver la televisión
3. **what kind?** ¿qué clase? ¿qué tipo?
   What kind of candy do you like? ¿Qué clase de dulces le gustan (*a usted*)? ¿Qué tipo de dulces le gustan (*a usted*)?
4. **all kinds** toda clase; de todo tipo
   I like all kinds of candy. Me gusta toda clase de dulces. Me gusta todo tipo de dulces.

5. **in the morning** en la mañana
6. **in the afternoon** en la tarde
7. **at night** en la noche, de noche
8. **The people are working.** La gente está trabajando.
9. **There was going to be time.** Iba a haber tiempo.
   There were going to be boys. Iba a haber muchachos.

EXERCISE 1
Traduzca las siguientes oraciones y practique leyéndolas.

1. There was always a car in the garage.
2. Was there always a car in the garage?
3. There were often three women there.
4. Were there often three women there?
5. My cousin wants to look for the book.
6. My cousin doesn't want to look for the book.
7. Does my cousin want to look for the book?
8. Doesn't my cousin want to look for the book?
9. The children are putting on their shoes.
10. The children aren't putting on their shoes.
11. Are the children putting on their shoes?
12. Aren't the children putting on their shoes?
13. My brother was forgetting everything.
14. My brother wasn't forgetting everything.
15. Was my brother forgetting everything?
16. Wasn't my brother forgetting everything?
17. John's friend is going to sleep here.
18. John's friend isn't going to sleep here.
19. Is John's friend going to sleep here?
20. Isn't John's friend going to sleep here?
21. The students want to ask a question.
22. The students don't want to ask a question.
23. Do the students want to ask a question?
24. Don't the students want to ask a question?

El tiempo pasado de los verbos regulares

El tiempo pasado en inglés corresponde en castellano al pretérito (miré, miraste, etc.; viví, viviste, etc.) y en ocasiones al copretérito (miraba, mirabas, etc.; vivía, vivías, etc.).

El tiempo pasado de los verbos regulares se forma agregando **ed** al infinitivo sin la partícula **to**. Si el verbo termina en **e**, solamente se agrega **d**. Ejemplos: **I looked (at)** (Yo miré, Yo miraba). **He lived** (Él vivió, Él vivía).

En el afirmativo del pasado la forma del verbo no sufre ningún cambio. Es igual en todas las personas. Estudie las siguientes formas.

I worked	yo trabajé, trabajaba
you worked	tú trabajaste, trabajabas
you worked	usted trabajó, trabajaba
he worked	él trabajó, trabajaba
she worked	ella trabajó, trabajaba
it worked	ello trabajó, trabajaba
we worked	trabajamos, trabajábamos
you worked	ustedes trabajaron, trabajaban
they worked	ellos trabajaron, trabajaban

La pronunciación de la terminación ed

Para la pronunciación de la terminación **ed** hay tres reglas:

1. Si el infinitivo termina en **d** o **t**, la terminación **ed** se pronuncia como una sílaba más, es decir **ed**.

visit	visited	want	wanted
wait (for)	waited (for)	need	needed

2. Si el infinitivo termina con sonido de **ch**, **f**, **k**, **p**, **s**, **sh**, **x**, la terminación **ed** se pronuncia como **t**, incorporando el sonido de la **t** en la pronunciación de la última sílaba, o bien, cuando el verbo conste de una sola sílaba, el sonido **t** se incorpora a esta misma.

laugh (at)	laughed (at)	walk	walked
ask	asked	help	helped
like	liked	wash	washed
look (at)	looked (at)	pass	passed
look (for)	looked (for)	finish	finished
talk	talked	fix	fixed
work	worked	watch	watched

3. En todos los otros casos la terminación **ed** se pronuncia como **d**, incorporando el sonido de la **d** en la pronunciación de la última sílaba, o bien cuando el verbo conste de una sola sílaba, el sonido **d** se incorpora a esta misma. Véase página 134 para entender mejor estas reglas gramaticales.

answer	answered	open	opened
call	called	turn on	turned on
clean	cleaned	turn off	turned off
learn	learned	study	studied
live	lived	use	used

EXERCISE 2
Traduzca las siguientes oraciones y practique leyéndolas.

1. I asked a lot of questions.
2. You finished at eight-thirty.
3. You fixed the radio.
4. He helped his father.
5. She laughed at the boys.
6. We liked it a lot.
7. They looked at the picture.
8. They passed by my house.
9. I talked to my friend.
10. You worked every afternoon.

11. She washed her dresses at night.
12. He walked home.
13. She visited her friend.
14. We waited every day.
15. You wanted to go home.
16. They answered the phone.
17. I called my sister.
18. You cleaned the kitchen.
19. You learned a lot of Spanish.
20. He lived in the United States.
21. She opened all the windows.
22. We studied everything.
23. You turned on the light.
24. They turned off the radio.
25. I used John's phone.
26. He needed a lot of things.
27. She liked to work.
28. They liked to go.
29. He wanted to come.
30. We wanted to wait.

EXERCISE 3

Llene los espacios con el tiempo pasado del verbo indicado y traduzca.

1. (ask) We _____ the teacher many questions.
2. (finish) The men _____ their work last night.
3. (laugh at) The children _____ the people in the store.
4. (look at) The women _____ the nice houses on that street.
5. (look for) John _____ his hat in the bedroom.
6. (fix) Mr. Johnson _____ the window in the bathroom.
7. (visit) I _____ Veracruz in January.
8. (wait for) My friend _____ me last night for an hour.
9. (want) Alice _____ to go to the movies.
10. (call) He _____ the boys yesterday.
11. (use) Miss Johnson _____ that book last year.
12. (turn on) We _____ the light at night.
13. (clean) My mother _____ the living room in the afternoon.
14. (open) Mrs. Carter _____ the windows and doors every morning.
15. (study) We _____ English every day.

El pasado de los verbos irregulares

No hay regla para saber cómo formar el pasado de los verbos irregulares.

Hay que aprender los verbos irregulares de memoria. Tanto para los verbos regulares como para los verbos irregulares no hay ningún cambio en la conjugación del pasado en afirmativo.

Present	Past	Present	Past
am, is, are	was, were	see	saw
bring	brought	sit (down)	sat (down)
come	came	sleep	slept
do	did	speak	spoke
eat	ate	take	took
feel	felt	teach	taught
forget	forgot	tell	told
get up	got up	think	thought
give	gave	think (about, of)	thought (about, of)
go	went		
go back	went back	know	knew
have	had	make	made
read	read	put	put
run	ran	put on	put on
wake up	woke up	say	said
wear	wore	understand	understood
write	wrote		

EXERCISE 4

Traduzca las siguientes oraciones y practique leyéndolas.

1. I was at home.
2. I brought it today.
3. You came yesterday.
4. She ate dinner.
5. He felt sick.
6. We forgot the money.
7. You got up early.
8. They gave their word.

9. She went to the movies.
10. You came on Tuesday.
11. He had the money.
12. She knew everything.
13. We knew that man.
14. She made a lot.
15. He put on his shoes.
16. They read the letter.
17. I said that.
18. You saw all the men.
19. She sat down.
20. They slept a lot.
21. She spoke English.
22. We took the notebooks.
23. You taught English.
24. I thought about you.
25. They understood Spanish.
26. He woke up at six-thirty.
27. She wore a dress.
28. We wrote a book.

EXERCISE 5

Llene los espacios con el tiempo pasado del verbo indicado y traduzca.

1. (see) I _____ that movie last week.
2. (bring) The two pictures that my uncle _____ from Mexico are on the wall.
3. (come) My aunt _____ to see me at five o'clock.
4. (eat) The boys _____ in the garden on Friday.
5. (say, feel) Mary _____ that she _____ sick last week.
6. (forget, put) I _____ to give you the money that I _____ on the table.
7. (get up) We _____ late on Sunday.
8. (give) He _____ me money for everything.
9. (go) The Carter Family _____ to the United States last month.
10. (have, come) Robert _____ ten suits when he _____ to Mexico the first time.
11. (speak, be) Alice _____ Spanish when she _____ in Mexico.
12. (understand, read) John and Robert _____ every word they _____ in that book.

13. (put on, run) The children _____ their shoes and _____ into the garden.
14. (sleep, wake up) I _____ for eight hours last night and _____ at seven-twenty.
15. (think, teach) He _____ of his cousin who _____ English in that school.
16. (make, wear) Mary _____ a new green dress and _____ it to school.
17. (write) Who _____ that letter?
18. (sit down, think) I _____ in that chair near the window and _____ about my work in the office.
19. (know) William _____ all the words.
20. (go back) Mrs. Davis _____ to Monterrey in July.

EXERCISE 6

Coloque los adverbios de frecuencia en su lugar correcto y traduzca.

1. (usually) Do you get up late on Sunday?
2. (sometimes) We went to the movies at night.
3. (seldom) He was late for his English class.
4. (always) They got up late in the morning.
5. (never) I spoke Spanish to my English teacher.
6. (ever) Do you speak Spanish to your teacher?
7. (sometimes) The children ate a lot.
8. (rarely) They visit their grandfather in the afternoon.
9. (often) They don't wear their new shoes and dresses.
10. (ever) Don't they clean the curtains and the rug?
11. (always) He is sick at night.
12. (ever) Weren't you in New York in January?
13. (never) They can get up before ten o'clock.
14. (often) Couldn't the boys go to the movies?
15. (ever) Do the children wash before they go to school?

EXERCISE 7
Práctica verbal

1. He always goes back early.
2. He doesn't always go back early.
3. Does he always go back early?
4. Doesn't he always go back early?
5. Why does he always go back early?
6. He went back early.
7. He usually went back early.
8. He rarely went back early.
9. He never went back early.
10. She's going to go back late.
11. She isn't going to go back late.
12. Is she going to go back late?
13. Isn't she going to go back late?
14. Why is she going to go back late?
15. They were going to go back at six.
16. They weren't going to go back at six.
17. Were they going to go back at six?
18. Weren't they going to go back at six?
19. Why were they going to go back at six?
20. He can go back home.
21. He can never go back home.
22. He can't ever go back home.
23. Can he ever go back home?
24. Can't he ever go back home?
25. Why can't he ever go back home?
26. He could go back home.
27. He could never go back home.
28. He couldn't ever go back home.
29. Could he ever go back home?
30. Couldn't he ever go back home?
31. Why couldn't he ever go back home?
32. He wants to go back in the morning.

33. He doesn't want to go back in the morning.
34. Does he want to go back in the morning?
35. Doesn't he want to go back in the morning?

EXERCISE 8
Práctica verbal. *Repita el ejercicio 7, usando formas de los verbos* **laugh at, pass, need, ask a question, watch TV** *en oraciones cortas. Emplee las palabras interrogativas* **when** *y* **why** *y los adverbios de frecuencia cuando sea posible.*

EXERCISE 9
Lea y traduzca estas oraciones y fechas.

1. Only two of the boys needed to bring their books.
2. What kind of dresses were those women looking for?
3. We saw all kinds of shoes, hats, and suits in the window of that store.
4. He wanted to put everything on the table, but he said he couldn't because the table was dirty.
5. I don't want to go back to the United States in December because it's very cold.
6. We laughed at William because he was looking for his hat in the bedroom, and it was in the living room.
7. If you aren't sick on Wednesday, are you going to the movies?
8. Each man said, "Thank you and good-bye", when he passed by the woman.
9. He couldn't answer all the questions in English, so he answered some of the questions in Spanish.
10. We knew that the tenth lesson was going to be very hard. That's why we studied for three hours.
11. I had many nice things to give the children—[1]all kinds of dresses and suits and a book for each one.

[1] En inglés, este guion, en ocasiones, hace las veces de los **:** en castellano.

12. Was it very cold in New York when you were there?
13. There was no room in the living room, and it was so hot in the dining room that we felt sick.
14. If we put all the things that Mr. Jackson needs on the table, he can fix the bathroom when he comes.
15. Is John's little brother too small to wear this suit that Robert's mother brought?
16. December 3, 1920. July 4, 1776. January 23, 1955. April 1, 1938. August 31, 1866. June 22, 1694. March 25, 1559. May 2, 1915. November 11, 1918. February 15, 1886.

on the 15th of September	on the 2nd of April
on the 30th of January	on the 1st of March
on the 12th of October	on the 3rd of November
on the 31st of July	on the 13th of September
on the 7th of May	on the 21st of June

EXERCISE 10
Escriba en inglés.

1. ¿Quién dijo que iba a hacer frío en abril?
2. Teníamos mucha hambre, pero no pudimos comer.
3. Él vivió y trabajó diez años en Estados Unidos.
4. Enrique me iba a visitar el quince de septiembre, pero no pudo.
5. ¿Qué hora es? No sé, pero es demasiado tarde para ir al parque.
6. Había toda clase de cosas bonitas en aquella tienda.
7. ¿Qué clase de vestido quiere (usted) llevar?
8. Ellos necesitaban diez hombres para hacer todo este trabajo.
9. Si Juan puede arreglar el coche, ¿por qué no podemos ir al cine?
10. Juan no pudo componer el coche. Por eso no pudimos ir al cine.

EXERCISE 11
Dictado

1. He fixed that table in the dining room, but we can't use it.
2. I passed by his house, but I couldn't see a light, so I don't think he was at home.
3. The boys laughed at the movie.
4. Miss Nelson went back home on the 4th of July.
5. It was very late. That's why we couldn't go to the movies.
6. If he comes early on Monday, we're going to look for all kinds of shoes.
7. I don't have to take my book because I know all the words in the lesson.
8. Mike said he knew that man when he lived in Texas.
9. The teacher gave each boy a pencil and each girl a pen.
10. Only ten boys could read the lesson because there were only five books.

EXERCISE 12
Conversación. *Conteste las siguientes preguntas.*

1. What kind of books do you like to read?
2. Do you like to see all kinds of movies?
3. What's your first name?
4. What's your last name?
5. How old are you?
6. When is your birthday?
7. What day was yesterday?
8. Were you watching TV last night?
9. Do you always watch TV?
10. Does he like to watch TV?
11. How many minutes are there in an hour?
12. How many hours are there in a day?

13. How many days are there in a week?
14. How many days are there in a year?
15. How many weeks are there in a year?
16. How many weeks are there in a month?
17. How many months are there in a year?

Conteste las siguientes preguntas en el afirmativo y en el negativo.

18. Do you go to the movies every day?
19. Do you see your cousin every morning?
20. Do you always bring your books to school?
21. Are you laughing at me?
22. Are they laughing at Mary?
23. Was there going to be time?
24. Were there going to be a lot of people?

Lesson 15

VOCABULARY

1. **to buy, bought** comprar, compró
2. **to sell, sold** vender, vendió
3. **to find, found** encontrar, encontró
4. **to begin, began** empezar, empezó
5. **to drink, drank** tomar, tomó; beber, bebió
6. **to get, got** conseguir, consiguió
7. **both** los dos, ambos
8. **about** como; acerca de; unos; aproximadamente
9. **same** mismo
10. **more** más
11. **almost** casi
12. **which** cuál
13. **breakfast** desayuno
14. **supper** cena, merienda
15. **soup** sopa
16. **milk** leche
17. **egg** huevo
18. **bread** pan
    a loaf of bread un pan (*de caja*)
19. **butter** mantequilla
20. **meat** carne

IDIOMS

1. When is your saint's day? ¿Cuándo es su santo?
2. What's the matter with John? ¿Qué pasa con Juan? ¿Qué tiene Juan?
3. What happened to John? ¿Qué pasó con Juan? ¿Qué le pasó a Juan?

LESSON 15

4. **Will you please...?** ¿(No) me quieres...?
   Will you please give me the book? ¿(No) me quieres dar el libro?
   Will you please do me a favor? ¿(No) me quieres hacer un favor?
5. **the day after tomorrow** pasado mañana
   the day before yesterday anteayer
6. **What did you say?** ¿Cómo dijo?
7. **to eat (have) breakfast** desayunar
8. **to eat (have) dinner** comer (*la comida principal*)
9. **to eat (have) supper** cenar, merendar

EXERCISE 1

Traduzca las siguientes oraciones y practique leyéndolas.

1. Laugh.
2. Don't laugh.
3. His brother seldom laughs.
4. His brother rarely laughs.
5. Does his brother often laugh?
6. Doesn't his brother often laugh?
7. His brother is going to fix the lights.
8. His brother isn't going to fix the lights.
9. Is his brother going to fix the lights?
10. Isn't his brother going to fix the lights?
11. Helen's sister was going to go back.
12. Helen's sister wasn't going to go back.
13. Was Helen's sister going to go back?
14. Wasn't Helen's sister going to go back?
15. They have to pass by my house.
16. They don't have to pass by my house.
17. Do they have to pass by my house?
18. Don't they have to pass by my house?
19. The boys needed money.
20. His brother laughed at me.

El pasado del verbo do

El pasado de las formas del verbo **do** se construye con la palabra **did**. **Did** corresponde al pasado de **hacer** cuando se usa como verbo principal. Ejemplos:

> I did the homework. We did the homework.
> Hice la tarea. Hicimos la tarea.

El auxiliar did

Como auxiliar, **did** se usa en preguntas y negaciones en pasado con todos los verbos, menos con las formas del verbo **be** y con otros auxiliares como **can** y **could**. **Did** sirve para todas las personas, y se usa con el infinitivo sin la partícula **to**.

La contracción negativa de **did not** es la palabra **didn't**.

Afirmativo

> **I wanted** yo quise, quería **it wanted** ello quiso
> **you wanted** tú quisiste **we wanted** nosotros quisimos
> **you wanted** usted quiso **you wanted** ustedes quisieron
> **he wanted** él quiso **they wanted** ellos quisieron
> **she wanted** ella quiso

Negativo

> **I didn't want** yo no quise, no quería **it didn't want** ello no quiso
> **you didn't want** tú no quisiste **we didn't want** nosotros no quisimos
> **you didn't want** usted no quiso **you didn't want** uestedes no quisieron
> **he didn't want** él no quiso **they didn't want** ellos no quisieron
> **she didn't want** ella no quiso

LESSON 15

Interrogativo

Recuerde el orden de las palabras para el interrogativo: auxiliar, sustantivo o pronombre, verbo.

did I want? ¿yo quise, quería?
did you want? ¿tú quisiste?
did you want? ¿usted quiso?
did he want? ¿él quiso?
did she want? ¿ella quiso?
did it want? ¿ello quiso?
did we want? ¿nosotros quisimos?
did you want? ¿ustedes quisieron?
did they want? ¿ellos quisieron?

Interrogativo negativo

didn't I want? ¿yo no quise, no quería?
didn't you want? ¿tú no quisiste?
didn't you want? ¿usted no quiso?
didn't he want? ¿él no quiso?
didn't she want? ¿ella no quiso?
didn't it want? ¿ello no quiso?
didn't we want? ¿nosoros no quisimos?
didn't you want? ¿ustedes no quisieron?
didn't they want? ¿ellos no quisieron?

EXERCISE 2
Práctica verbal

1. He brought the books.
2. He didn't bring the books.
3. Did he bring the books?
4. Didn't he bring the books?
5. Why did he bring the books?
6. Why didn't he bring the books?

EXERCISE 3
Práctica verbal. *Repita el ejercicio 2, usando formas de los verbos* **answer, ask, say, run, speak, go, think, sleep, know** *en oraciones cortas. Emplee un sustantivo o pronombre distinto con cada verbo. Use las palabras interrogativas cuando sea posible.*

EXERCISE 4
Traduzca estas oraciones. Cámbielas al pasado y traduzca.

1. He doesn't say the same thing.
2. Do you talk about your friend's new car?
3. Which boy do you see at the movies?
4. Does he know all the lesson?
5. The boys don't have the same last name.
6. We don't like to get up early.
7. Those girls don't want a lot.
8. They don't wear their hats to the movies.
9. Robert and John don't eat dinner early.
10. Mary and Alice don't think of their parents.

EXERCISE 5
Traduzca estas oraciones. Cámbielas al negativo, interrogativo e interrogativo negativo.

1. I worked in the office.
2. He ate the bread.
3. She waited for her mother.
4. We sat in the living room.
5. They taught English.
6. You understood the teacher.
7. Mr. Hunt read the lesson.
8. Mrs. Smith put on her hat.
9. Miss Carson had a new dress.
10. Mary looked at everything.

El tiempo pasado de la expresión idiomática de necesidad

El pasado de la expresión idiomática de necesidad se forma con **had** (el pasado de **have**), seguido de un infinitivo con la partícula **to**. Equivale al pasado de **tener que**, seguido de un infinitivo. Compare el inglés con el español.

Afirmativo

| I had to go. | Tuve, tenía que ir. |
| We had to work. | Tuvimos, teníamos que trabajar. |

Negativo

| He didn't have to come. | Él no tuvo, tenía que venir. |
| They didn't have to speak. | Ellos no tuvieron, tenían que hablar. |

Interrogativo

Recuerde el orden de las palabras para el interrogativo: auxiliar, sustantivo o pronombre, verbo.

Auxiliar	Sustantivo o pronombre	Verbo
Did	you	have to work?
¿Tenías	(tú)	que trabajar?
Did	we	have to go?
¿Tuvimos	(nosotros)	que ir?

Interrogativo negativo

Auxiliar	Sustantivo o pronombre	Verbo
Didn't	Bill	have to eat?
¿No tenía	Bill	que comer?
Didn't	he	have to go?
¿No tuvo	él	que ir?

EXERCISE 6
Práctica verbal

1. You had to go.
2. You didn't have to go.
3. Did you have to go?
4. Didn't you have to go?
5. Why did you have to go?
6. Why didn't you have to go?

EXERCISE 7
Práctica verbal. *Repita el ejercicio 6, usando formas de los verbos* **do, come, know, finish, feel, give** *en oraciones cortas. Emplee un sustantivo o pronombre distinto con cada verbo. Use las palabras interrogativas cuando sea posible.*

EXERCISE 8
Llene los espacios con los infinitivos indicados y traduzca.

1. (to finish) I had _____ my work at five o'clock.
2. (to open) He had _____ the door every morning.
3. (to make) She had _____ four dresses last week.
4. (to look for) We had _____ the money.
5. (to help) The boys had _____ the teacher.
6. (to turn off) My grandmother had _____ the light at nine o'clock.
7. (to sleep) The child had _____ on the hard bed.

8. (to study)   Those verbs that we had _____ were easy.
9. (to read)   The girls had _____ the same lesson yesterday.
10. (to tell)   Mr. Carson had _____ the boys about his work in the office.

EXERCISE 9

Traduzca estas oraciones. Cámbielas al negativo, interrogativo e interrogativo negativo.

1. They had to live in a small house.
2. They had to learn all the hard verbs.
3. She had to put on her green dress.
4. He had to wear his new suit.
5. I had to wash a lot of dresses.
6. We had to wake up at six o'clock.
7. You had to write a letter to your friend.
8. John had to go to the movies on Thursday.
9. Mrs. Burns had to work every day last week.
10. Mr. Burns had to call the children.

EXERCISE 10
Práctica verbal

1. He always buys bread.
2. He doesn't always buy bread.
3. Does he always buy bread?
4. Doesn't he always buy bread?
5. Why does he always buy bread?
6. He sometimes bought bread.
7. He didn't ever buy bread.
8. Did he sometimes buy bread?
9. Didn't he ever buy bread?

10. How much bread did he buy?
11. He's buying milk.
12. He isn't buying milk.
13. Is he buying milk?
14. Isn't he buying milk?
15. Where's he buying milk?
16. He was going to buy milk.
17. He wasn't going to buy milk.
18. Was he going to buy milk?
19. Wasn't he going to buy milk?
20. Where was he going to buy milk?
21. He can usually buy meat.
22. He can't usually buy meat.
23. Can he usually buy meat?
24. Can't he usually buy meat?
25. Where can he usually buy meat?
26. He liked to buy candy.
27. He didn't like to buy candy.
28. Did he like to buy candy?
29. Didn't he like to buy candy?
30. Where did he like to buy candy?
31. He has to buy a book.
32. He doesn't have to buy a book.
33. Does he have to buy a book?
34. Doesn't he have to buy a book?
35. How many books does he have to buy?

EXERCISE 11

Práctica verbal. *Repita el ejercicio 10, usando formas de los verbos* **sell, drink, find, begin, get, eat (have) breakfast, eat (have) dinner, eat (have) supper** *en oraciones cortas. Emplee un sustantivo o pronombre distinto con cada verbo y los adverbios de frecuencia cuando pueda. Use las palabras interrogativas* **what, where, how many, how much** *cuando sea posible.*

EXERCISE 12
Lea y traduzca las siguientes oraciones.

1. We bought milk and eggs for breakfast, but we didn't buy bread and butter because we forgot to take all the money.
2. I bought a lot of meat in that store the day before yesterday.
3. Did both boys go to the movies on Sunday afternoon?
4. I sold my old book for $1.50 (a dollar fifty) and bought a new book for $2.00 (two dollars).
5. She needed more milk for the soup, but she didn't want to buy it in that store.
6. Do you want to buy a loaf of bread?
7. I had to get about twenty Coca-Colas for dinner.
8. Almost all the boys had to buy new shoes before they went to the United States.
9. Didn't Mrs. Carter drink that water that was in the kitchen?
10. Where were you going when I saw you the day before yesterday?
11. We looked for the money that you put on the table in the dining room, but we couldn't find it.
12. Robert didn't get up early this morning because he didn't have to work.
13. I asked the old man what happened, but he said he couldn't tell me.
14. Was the boy's saint's day on Tuesday?
15. You don't have to look for my hat because I found it in the bedroom.
16. Miss Wells began her work at ten o'clock, but she didn't finish before dinner.
17. He didn't have breakfast, so he ate dinner early.
18. You didn't have to eat that meat if you didn't want it.

EXERCISE 13
Escriba en inglés.

1. Juan dijo que no tenía que trabajar en el día de su santo.
2. ¿Qué pasó con Juan? No sé, pero creo que está enfermo.
3. ¿No me quieres encender la luz?
4. ¿Por qué no vino él? Dijo que hoy quería cenar con mi papá.
5. Si él empieza pasado mañana, puede terminar el martes.
6. La señora Hall compró huevos, leche, un pan y mantequilla para el desayuno.
7. ¿Qué hacías cuando te vi antier? Yo estaba desayunando.
8. Había unos veinticuatro muchachos que no trajeron sus libros a la escuela.
9. Él dijo que podía venir el 16 de septiembre pero que no podía traer a su esposa.
10. No fui a Estados Unidos en marzo. Fui en abril.

EXERCISE 14
Dictado

1. Is your saint's day on the 21st of July?
2. Is your birthday on the 3rd of February?
3. What's the matter with that child?
4. Will you do me a favor and bring me the pencil I put on the kitchen table?
5. It's almost time to begin work.
6. Both of these eggs are bad.
7. I had to say the same word five times.
8. Did you drink milk when you had breakfast?
9. He said he didn't have time to study his lesson.
10. The first lesson was easy, but the second was hard.

EXERCISE 15

Conversación. *Conteste las siguientes preguntas.*

1. When is your saint's day?
2. When is your birthday?
3. How old are you?
4. What's the matter with you?
5. What happened to you yesterday?

Conteste las siguientes preguntas en afirmativo y en negativo.

6. Did you ask the teacher?
7. Did you answer the question in English?
8. Did he bring the eggs?
9. Did he sometimes come on the 1st of May?
10. Did she always call her brother?
11. Did she usually clean the bedroom?
12. Did they eat breakfast?
13. Did John eat supper late?
14. Did you finish the book?
15. Did you buy a lot of meat?
16. Did you eat dinner early?
17. Did they go to the movies on Sunday night?
18. Did John get up early?
19. Did Robert give the money to the teacher?
20. Did Mary go back to Monterrey?
21. Did Alice ever help the boys?
22. Did Mr. Jackson and I have the money?
23. Did George and I know the lesson?
24. Did you and Helen laugh at me?
25. Did the boys laugh at me?

Lesson 16

VOCABULARY

1. **to leave, left** dejar, dejó; salir (de), salió (de); irse, se fue
2. **to jump, jumped** saltar, saltó
3. **to get angry (at), got angry (at),** enojarse (con), se enojó (con)
4. **to get mad (at), got mad (at),** enojarse (con), se enojó (con)
5. **to come back, came back** regresar, regresó (*de allá para acá*)
6. **to lie down, lay down** recostarse, se recostó; echarse, se echó
7. **to stand up, stood up** ponerse de pie, se puso de pie
8. **all that** todo lo que
9. **other, others** otro, otros
10. **tired** cansado
11. **later** más tarde
12. **selfish** (*adj.*) egoísta
13. **asleep** dormido
14. **comfortable** cómodo
15. **chicken** pollo
16. **dog** perro
17. **cow** vaca
18. **barn** granero
19. **manger** pesebre
20. **hay** heno
21. **place** lugar
22. **field** campo
23. **story** cuento; historia

IDIOMS

1. **Lie down.** Recuéstate, Échate.
2. **Stand up.** Póngase de pie, Levántese.
3. **Get out of here.** Vete de aquí, Lárgate de aquí.
4. **Leave me alone.** Déjame en paz.
5. **I don't care.** No me importa, Me es indiferente.
6. **He's standing (up).** Él está parado.
7. **He's lying down.** Él está recostado.
8. **to be mad (at)** estar enojado (con)
   to be angry (at) estar enojado (con)
9. **She's mad (angry) at me.** Está enojada conmigo.

EXERCISE 1
Traduzca las siguientes oraciones y practique leyéndolas.

1. Buy my supper.
2. Don't buy my supper.
3. Her brother bought my supper.
4. Her brother didn't buy my supper.
5. His sister had to buy my supper.
6. His sister didn't have to buy my supper.
7. My father sold your car.
8. My father didn't sell your car.
9. Your sister drank a lot of milk.
10. Your sister didn't drink a lot of milk.
11. Did your sister drink a lot of milk?
12. Didn't your sister drink a lot of milk?
13. When did your sister drink a lot of milk?
14. Their sister wanted a lot.
15. Their sister didn't want a lot.
16. Did their sister want a lot?
17. Didn't their sister want a lot?
18. Why didn't their sister want a lot?
19. Our mother had to buy a loaf of bread.
20. Our mother didn't have to buy a loaf of bread.

Los pronombres objetivos

Los pronombres objetivos se colocan después de los verbos y las preposiciones. Apréndalos y fíjese que en el nominativo y el objetivo son iguales los pronombres **it** y **you**.

Nominativo	Objetivo	
I	**me**	me
you	**you**	te, le, lo, la
he	**him**	le, lo
she	**her**	le, la
it	**it**	lo, la
we	**us**	nos
you	**you**	les, los, las
they	**them**	les, los, las

Pronombres objetivos usados después de verbos

1. I saw **him**.
2. He helped **you**.
3. They told **you**.
4. We asked **them**.
5. They called **us**.
6. My sister visited **her**.
7. You took **it**.
8. The teacher answered **me**.

Pronombres objetivos usados después de preposiciones

1. The child went with **her**.
2. She looked at **me**.
3. They spoke to **us**.
4. We talked to **them**.
5. He gave the money to **her**.
6. The boys laughed at **him**.
7. You looked for **it**.
8. My brother waited for **you**.

EXERCISE 2
Llene los espacios con el pronombre de objeto entre paréntesis y traduzca.

1. Why did you take (he) _____ to school so late?
2. The teacher read (she) _____ a book in English, but she didn't understand (it) _____.
3. I gave (you) _____ and John the money to buy the bread.
4. My brother didn't wait for (he) _____.
5. Henry was going to help (they) _____, but he didn't have time.
6. He asked (I) _____ the time.
7. My father said that he was going to buy that car for (we) _____.
8. I'm mad at (he) _____, and he knows (it) _____.
9. Please call (I) _____ on Friday.
10. The rug was dirty, so I cleaned (it) _____.
11. The boys laughed at (she) _____ because she sat down in the water.
12. They looked at (we) _____ when they saw (we) _____, but they didn't speak to (we) _____.
13. When I saw (you) _____ on the street, you were with (they) _____.
14. Don't give (it) _____ to (they) _____; give (it) _____ to (I) _____.
15. I waited for (you) _____ for twenty minutes, but you didn't come, so I went with (she) _____.

EXERCISE 3

Llene los espacios con la forma objetiva del pronombre que corresponde al sustantivo entre paréntesis y traduzca.

*Ejemplo: He visits (his aunt) every week. He visits **her** every week.*

1. I can see (my mother) _____ in the garden.
2. He couldn't find (my sister) _____ at the movies.
3. John fixed (the car) _____ and put (the car) _____ in the garage.
4. I saw (my uncle) _____ yesterday.
5. We bought (the chairs) _____ for $25.00 (dollars).
6. Mrs. Carter gave (John) _____ a new hat.
7. They looked at (Henry) _____ and (Alice) _____.
8. I answered (the teacher) _____ in Spanish.
9. Mary gave (the books) _____ to the boys.
10. I told (the boys) _____ that I was mad.
11. Please don't talk to (John and me) _____ now.
12. If you want to wait for (my father and me) _____, we can go with you.
13. Mr. Smith put (the cow and the dog) _____ in the barn.
14. He got mad at (John) _____, not at (Alice) _____.
15. What are the girls going to do with (that dirty dress) _____?

Like con los sustantivos y pronombres objetivos

El verbo **like** se conjuga en inglés como cualquier otro verbo. Cuando no está seguido de una forma verbal, lo estará por un sustantivo o pronombre objetivo que se referirá a un sustantivo ya mencionado o sobreentendido. Estudie los ejemplos.

I like Mary.
Me gusta María.

I like her.
Me gusta (ella a mí)

I like you.
Me simpatizas.

You like John.
(a usted) Le gusta Juan.

You like him.
Le gusta (él a usted)

He likes the house.
(a él) Le gusta la casa.

He likes it.
Le gusta.

She likes these boys.
(a ella) Le simpatizan estos muchachos.

She likes them.
Le simpatizan (a ella)

He likes those girls.
(a él) Le gustan esas muchachas.

He likes them.
Le gustan (a él)

We like these dogs.
Nos gustan estos perros.

We like them.
Nos gustan.

You like the teachers.
(a ustedes) Les simpatizan los profesores.

You like them.
Les simpatizan (a ustedes)

They like Mexico.
(a ellos, ellas) Les gusta México.

They like it.
Les gusta (a ellos, ellas)

They like you and Mary.
(a ellos, ellas) Les gustan usted y María.

They like you.
Les gustan (ustedes a ellos, ellas)

EXERCISE 4

Llene los espacios con la forma objetiva del pronombre que corresponde al sustantivo entre paréntesis y traduzca.

1. I like (this girl) _____ a lot.
2. Do you like (the house) _____?
3. He says that he likes (John) _____.
4. I know that he's going to like (the girls) _____.
5. The teacher likes (you and me) _____.
6. Helen said that she liked (Paul and you) _____.
7. Does he like (his new shoes) _____?
8. Did you like (that story) _____?
9. Do they like (my sister) _____?
10. They aren't going to like (these books) _____.
11. They don't have to like (Peter and me) _____.
12. Bill is going to like (your uncle) _____ a lot.
13. Is he going to like (my aunt) _____ too?
14. Do you like (my new car) _____?
15. Do they like (the United States) _____?

El imperativo

Como ya sabe, el imperativo de la segunda persona singular y plural **you** (tú, usted, ustedes) se forma con el infinitivo sin la partícula **to**, suprimiendo el pronombre.

El imperativo con todas las otras personas se forma con la palabra **let**, seguida del pronombre objetivo, o del sustantivo y el infinitivo del verbo empleado sin la partícula **to**. Estudie los siguientes ejemplos y fíjese en las dos formas de la primera persona plural (**let us** y **let's**) y sus traducciones correspondientes.

Let me answer.   Que conteste yo, Déjeme contestar.
Answer.   Contesta (tú), Conteste (usted).

LESSON 16

Let him answer.	Que conteste él, Déjelo contestar.
Let John answer.	Que conteste Juan, Deje que Juan conteste.
Let her answer.	Que conteste ella, Déjela contestar.
Let Mary answer.	Que conteste María, Deje que María conteste.
Let us answer.	Déjenos contestar.
Let's answer.	Contestemos, Vamos a contestar.
Answer.	Contesten (ustedes).
Let them answer.	Que contesten ellos (ellas). Déjelos (las) contestar.
Let the boys answer.	Que contesten los muchachos. Deje que contesten los muchachos.
Don't let me answer.	Que no conteste yo, No me deje contestar.
Don't answer.	No contestes, No conteste.
Don't let him answer.	Que no conteste él, No lo dejes contestar.
Don't let John answer.	Que no conteste Juan, No deje que Juan conteste.
Don't let her answer.	Que no conteste ella, No deje que ella conteste.
Don't let Mary answer.	Que no conteste María, No deje que María conteste.
Don't let us answer.	No nos deje contestar.
Let's not answer.	No contestemos, No vayamos a contestar.
Don't answer.	No contesten (ustedes).
Don't let them answer.	Que no contesten ellos (ellas), No los (las) deje que contesten.
Don't let the boys answer.	Que no contesten los muchachos, No deje que los muchachos contesten.

EXERCISE 5
Traduzca las siguientes oraciones.

1. Déjela venir.
2. No me deje venir.
3. Que venga él.
4. No lo deje venir.
5. Deje venir a mi hermana.
6. No deje que venga mi hermana.
7. Déjela venir.
8. No la deje venir.
9. Dejen que venga nuestra hermana.
10. No dejen que nuestra hermana venga.
11. Vengamos temprano.
12. No vengamos temprano.
13. Déjenos venir.
14. No nos deje venir.
15. Que vengan ellos.
16. Que no vengan ellos.
17. Dejen que vengan mis padres.
18. No dejen que vengan mis padres.
19. Déjeme comer.
20. No me deje comer.
21. Que coma él.
22. Que no coma él.
23. Deje que el perro coma.
24. No deje que el perro coma.
25. Déjenla comer.
26. No la dejen comer.
27. Vamos a comer (comamos).
28. No comamos.
29. Déjenos comer.
30. No nos deje comer.
31. No los deje comer.

El uso del gerundio con preposiciones

En castellano se usa un infinitivo después de las preposiciones. En inglés es preciso usar el gerundio (la forma **ing** del verbo). Note:

before going	antes de ir
without going	sin ir
after coming	después de venir
besides coming	además de venir

Aprenda las siguientes preposiciones.

beside	al lado de	**behind**	detrás de
besides	además de	**near**	cerca de
far from	lejos de	**next to**	junto a
in front of	delante de, enfrente de		

EXERCISE 6
Llene los espacios con la preposición correcta y traduzca.

1. My uncle sat (al lado de) _____ my father at the movies.
2. My uncle sat (junto a) _____ my father at the movies.
3. My uncle sat (delante de) _____ my father at the movies.
4. My uncle sat (lejos de) _____ my father at the movies.
5. My uncle sat (cerca de) _____ my father at the movies.
6. My uncle sat (detrás de) _____ my father at the movies.
7. (además de trabajar) _____ in an office, I teach English.
8. Henry was standing (enfrente de) _____ the house when you came.
9. Mary doesn't like to sit (cerca de) _____ the window because it's cold.
10. He saw your shoes (detrás de) _____ the sofa.
11. (Además de) _____ chicken, I ate candy.
12. (Después de comer) _____, we went to school.

13. We live (lejos de) _____ Mexico City.
14. Is Cuernavaca (lejos de) _____ Mexico City?
15. Please don't stand (al lado de) _____ me.
16. Is that your car (enfrente de) _____ the office?
17. Why are you standing (detrás de) _____ all those people?
18. Is there a school (cerca de) _____ your house?
19. The barn isn't very (lejos de) _____ the house.
20. If you stand (detrás de) _____ him, they can't see you.
21. (Además de comprar) _____ this green pencil, I bought a red book.
22. Come over here and sit (al lado de) _____ me.
23. (Además de) _____ getting up early, I have to work late at night.
24. Put your hat (al lado de) _____ Mary's books.
25. She lay down for an hour (antes de lavar) _____ the curtains.

EXERCISE 7
Práctica verbal

1. They always come back late.
2. They don't always come back late.
3. Do they always come back late?
4. Don't they always come back late?
5. Why do they always come back late?
6. They often came back late.
7. They didn't often come back late.
8. Did they often come back late?
9. Didn't they often come back late?
10. Why did they often come back late?
11. They're going to come back soon.

LESSON 16 167

12. They aren't going to come back soon.
13. Are they going to come back soon?
14. Aren't they going to come back soon?
15. Why aren't they going to come back soon?
16. They were going to come back soon.
17. They weren't going to come back soon.
18. Were they going to come back soon?
19. Weren't they going to come back soon?
20. What time were they going to come back?
21. They could come back on Tuesday.
22. They couldn't come back on Tuesday.
23. Could they come back on Tuesday?
24. Couldn't they come back on Tuesday?
25. What time could they come back on Tuesday?
26. They want to come back before six.
27. They don't want to come back before six.
28. Do they want to come back before six?
29. Don't they want to come back before six?
30. Why don't they want to come back before six?
31. They had to come back last night.
32. They didn't have to come back last night.
33. Did they have to come back last night?
34. Didn't they have to come back last night?
35. Why didn't they have to come back last night?

EXERCISE 8

Práctica verbal. *Repita el ejercicio 7, usando formas de los verbos* **leave, jump, get angry (at), get mad (at), be angry (at), be mad (at), come back, lie down, stand up** *en oraciones cortas. Emplee un sustantivo o pronombre distinto con cada verbo. Use los adverbios de frecuencia y las palabras interrogativas* **when** *y* **what time** *cuando sea posible.*

EXERCISE 9
Lea y traduzca.

The dog in the manger

One warm day a dog was looking for a comfortable place to sleep.

He looked in the barn and saw some hay in a cow's manger. The dog knew that the hay was the cow's supper; but he jumped into (al) the manger, lay down on the hay, and was soon asleep.

Sometime later the cow, tired and hungry, came back from the field where she had to work all day. She was thinking of the good supper she was going to find in the manger; but when she saw the dog lying on the hay, she didn't know what to do.

"Wake up", the cow said to the dog. "I worked all day, and I'm very hungry. Let me eat my supper."

The dog got angry because the cow woke him up. He stood up in the manger and said to the cow, "Get out of here and leave me alone. I don't care if this is your hay. I'm going to sleep here".

The cow said, "You can't eat my hay, and you don't want me to eat it. Why don't you let others have what you can't use? You're very selfish".

EXERCISE 10
Escriba en inglés.

1. ¿Me quieres hacer un favor? Con mucho gusto. ¿Qué puedo hacer?
2. Cuando el profesor dijo "Levántense" todos los muchachos se levantaron.
3. Antes de recostarme, voy a leer como una hora.
4. Vete de aquí y déjame en paz.
5. No me importa. Voy a regresar el lunes.

6. Él se puso tan furioso con aquel perro que quería venderlo.
7. Recuéstate en el piso. No hay lugar en la cama.
8. Ellos tienen toda clase de zapatos aquí. ¿Qué clase va a comprar usted?
9. Regresemos temprano porque estoy muy cansado.
10. Lo siento, pero no me puedo sentar junto a usted cuando comamos hoy.
11. Después de ir al cine, tomamos nuestra merienda.

EXERCISE 11
Dictado

1. I said, "Get out of the house and go to work".
2. Don't get mad at me.
3. Did you leave your car in front of my house last night?
4. Why did he have to come back on Wednesday?
5. He was so sick that he had to lie down.
6. Some of the boys stood up, and the others sat down.
7. Did he leave the other book here for me?
8. Yes, he left it on the table in the living room.
9. Besides putting hay in the barn for the cow, I had to give the dog his meat.
10. Is the field far from here? No, it's behind the barn.

EXERCISE 12
Conversación. *Conteste las siguientes preguntas.*

1. When is your saint's day?
2. When is your birthday?
3. How old are you?
4. What's your name?
5. What time is it?

Conteste las siguientes preguntas en el afirmativo y en el negativo.

6. Is the barn behind the house?
7. Is the house far from the barn?
8. Is the car in front of the house?
9. Is the store next to the house?
10. Is the store beside the house?
11. Is the store near the house?
12. Did you sit next to John?
13. Did you sit beside John?
14. Did you sit in front of John?
15. Did you sit far from John?
16. Did you sit behind John?
17. Did you sit near John?
18. Did you have two more books besides these?
19. Did the dog jump into (at) the cow's manger?
20. Did the dog lie down?
21. Do you ever get angry?
22. Do you ever get mad?
23. Do you like to stand up?
24. Do you want to sit down?
25. Do you want to lie down?
26. Do you like him?
27. Does he like her?
28. Do you like them?
29. Does she like it?
30. Did you like her very much?
31. Did he like it?
32. Did your mother like him?
33. Did she like the curtains?
34. Did Bob's sister like the movies?
35. Did you like the United States?
36. Was there a lot of time?
37. Weren't there a lot of chickens?
38. Is there going to be a lot of water?
39. Is it going to be cold?
40. Are you going to be thirty-six in October?

Lesson 17

VOCABULARY

1. **to invite, invited** invitar, invitó
2. **to meet, met** encontrar (se), se encontró (*personas o cosas por casualidad*); conocer, conoció (*personas o cosas por primera vez*)
3. **to set, set** colocar, colocó
4. **to hear, heard** oír, oyó
5. **to reply, replied** contestar, contestó
6. **shallow** poco profundo; extendido
7. **narrow** estrecho
8. **tall** (*estatura*) alto
9. **long** largo
10. **interesting** interesante
11. **fox** zorro
12. **stork** cigüeña
13. **plate** plato
14. **glass** vaso; vidrio; cristal
15. **mouth** boca; pico; hocico
16. **bill** pico
17. **knife** cuchillo
18. **knives** cuchillos
19. **fork** tenedor
20. **spoon** cuchara

IDIOMS

1. **to set the table, set the table** poner la mesa
2. **Come in.** Pase usted. (*de allá para acá*)
   Go in. Pase usted. (*de acá para allá*)
3. **That's all right.** No tenga cuidado, Está bien.

4. **It doesn't matter.** No le hace, No importa.
   It doesn't make any difference. No le hace, No importa.
5. **as far as I know** que yo sepa
6. **a little (milk)** un poco (de leche)
   a few (men) unos cuantos, unos pocos (hombres)
7. **to say good-bye (to)** despedirse (de)
   He said good-bye (to her). Se despidió (de ella).
8. **to get to** llegar a
   He got to Mexico at six. Llegó a México a las seis.
   to get here (there) llegar aquí (ahí)
   He got here (there) early. Llegó temprano.
   (Cuando no se indica el lugar a donde se llega, se debe emplear **here** o **there**, según el caso.)

EXERCISE 1
Traduzca estas oraciones y practique leyéndolas.

1. Stand up.
2. Don't stand up.
3. Let me lie down.
4. Don't let me lie down.
5. Let him lie down.
6. Don't let him lie down.
7. Let her lie down.
8. Don't let her lie down.
9. Let's lie down.
10. Let's not lie down.
11. Let us lie down.
12. Don't let us lie down.
13. Let them lie down.
14. Don't let them lie down.
15. Mr. Flint often gets mad.
16. Mr. Flint doesn't often get mad.
17. Does Mr. Flint often get mad?
18. Doesn't Mr. Flint often get mad?
19. Mr. Flint got mad at me.
20. Mr. Flint didn't get mad at me.

Los pronombres posesivos

Aprenda los pronombres posesivos. En inglés no se usa el artículo antes de los pronombres posesivos.

mine	el mío, la mía, los míos, las mías
yours	el tuyo, la tuya, los tuyos, las tuyas
yours	(de usted) el suyo, la suya, los suyos, las suyas
his	(de él) el suyo, la suya, los suyos, las suyas
hers	(de ella) el suyo, la suya, los suyos, las suyas
ours	el nuestro, la nuestra, los nuestros, las nuestras
yours	(de ustedes) el suyo, la suya, los suyos, las suyas
theirs	(de ellos, ellas) el suyo, la suya, los suyos, las suyas

EXERCISE 2

Llene los espacios con el pronombre posesivo que corresponde a las palabras entre paréntesis y traduzca.

1. Henry forgot his hat, so he wore (my hat) _____.
2. She has (her book) _____. Why don't you have (your book) _____?
3. John found his money, but George can't find (his money) _____.
4. Alice has her English lesson in the morning, but we have (our lesson) _____ in the afternoon.
5. I gave the money to Mr. Smith because it's (his money) _____.
6. This book isn't (my book) _____. It's (her book) _____.
7. I saw my mother at the movies, but I didn't see (his mother) _____.

LESSON 17

8. My car is in the garage. Can we go in (your car) _____?
9. That isn't our car. (our car) _____ is green.
10. If you can't find your pencil, the girls can give you (their pencil) _____.
11. This knife isn't (my knife) _____. It's (his knife) _____.
12. I work in my office, and he works in (his office) _____.
13. I don't want to read this book. I want to read (her book) _____.
14. I have your book, and you have (my book) _____.
15. If I can't find my pencil, I'm going to take (their pencil) _____.
16. This book isn't (your book) _____. It's (their book) _____.
17. She's going to wash her dress. Are you going to wash (your dress) _____ too?
18. My children are in the garden, but I don't see (your children) _____.
19. I'm going to ask him if he can fix (my radio) _____. Do you think he can fix (your radio) _____ too?
20. I turned off all my lights, but I didn't turn off (your lights) _____.

Much, many, little, few

Aprenda estas palabras.

Singular		Plural	
much	mucho	**many**	muchos
little	poco	**few**	pocos

Se usan las palabras **much** (mucho) y **little** (poco) antes de los sustantivos en singular. **Many** (muchos) y **few** (pocos) se usan antes de los sustantivos en plural. Recuerde el uso de los modismos **too much**, **too many** (pág. 44) y **so much**, **so many** (pág. 55).

EXERCISE 3
*Llene los espacios con **much, many** o **little, few**.*

1. We don't have (much, many) _____ time.
2. How (much, many) _____ money do you have?
3. How (much, many) _____ children do you have?
4. There isn't (much, many) _____ water in the kitchen.
5. There are (much, many) _____ books on the table.
6. Put a (little, few) _____ more milk in my glass.
7. Only a (little, few) _____ men worked yesterday.
8. There were so (little, few) _____ clean knives and forks in the kitchen that my wife couldn't set the table.
9. Of course, my husband is going to give you a (little, few) _____ more time.
10. That school is very big, but they have (little, few) _____ teachers.
11. I came to buy some books. How (much, many) _____ do you have?
12. I can't sleep well at night if I eat too (many, much) _____.
13. We're going to the United States in a (little, few) _____ days.
14. My husband has a (little, few) _____ old suits that he can give you.
15. Some of the boys were speaking English, but (much, many) _____ of them were speaking Spanish.
16. There was only a (little, few) _____ hay in the barn for the cows.
17. Some day, when I have only a (little, few) _____ work, I'm going to finish that book.
18. He didn't go to the movies because there were so (many, much) _____ people there.
19. We did so (many much) _____ work today that I'm very tired.
20. A (little, few) _____ of the girls wanted to go to the movies, but (many, much) _____ others wanted to go to Mary's house.

To say, to tell

Se traducen los infinitivos **to say** y **to tell** como decir, pero hay una diferencia en el uso de los dos.

Generalmente se usan formas del verbo **tell** cuando sigue un pronombre, un sustantivo o un pronombre de objeto. Cuando ninguno de ellos sigue, entonces se utilizan formas del verbo **say**. Si el verbo va seguido de una preposición, también se emplean formas del verbo **say**. Cuando uno vaya a citar las palabras exactas de una persona, se usa el verbo **say**, ya sea solo, o seguido de una frase con la preposición **to**. Estudie los ejemplos.

1. I told him that I was going to put the book on the table.
2. He said, "I'm fine".
3. He said to me, "I'm fine".
4. She says that she can't go.
5. Did he tell John that he is sick?

EXERCISE 4
Llene los espacios con la forma correcta de los verbos **tell** *y* **say** *y traduzca.*

1. What did he _____ you?
2. He _____ that he was going to study.
3. Why did Mary _____ that?
4. When they came in, they _____, "Good morning".
5. What are you going _____ your mother?
6. Are you going _____ her that you're sick?
7. No, I'm not going _____ my mother that I'm sick.
8. Why did you _____ me that?

9. We _____ Mary and Alice everything.
10. Don't _____ me.
11. He _____ that he was going _____ my father, but he didn't _____ him.
12. I didn't _____ that I didn't want to go. I _____ that I couldn't go.
13. I don't know why you _____ that.
14. When I see them, I'm going _____ them what you said.
15. What did he _____ you? He _____ us that it was time to eat.
16. I don't want _____ John that he can't go.
17. She only _____ that we needed a telephone.
18. Didn't you _____ us that your name was Robert?
19. We couldn't hear what the teacher was _____.
20. What did you _____?

Preposiciones

Aprenda estas preposiciones.

until	hasta *(empleado con tiempo)*
as far as	hasta *(empleado con distancia)*
above	arriba, arriba de
over	directamente encima de
below	abajo, debajo de
under	directamente debajo de
close	cerca
close to	cerca de
near	cerca, cerca de
toward	hacia
all over	por todo

EXERCISE 5
Llene los espacios con la preposición correcta y traduzca.

1. I waited for you (hasta) _____ four o'clock, but you didn't come.
2. Put your chair (cerca de) _____ mine.
3. They walked (hacia) _____ the city.
4. The light (de arriba de) _____ the table isn't very good.
5. Mr. Rogers lives (abajo de) _____ me on the third floor.
6. We sat very (cerca de) _____ the teacher, but we couldn't hear.
7. I'm not going to go (hasta) _____ tomorrow.
8. They could see the city (abajo de) _____ them.
9. (que yo sepa) _____ I know, he didn't work yesterday.
10. Mother put the picture on the wall (arriba de) _____ the sofa.
11. Fred found his shoes (debajo de) _____ the bed.
12. That dog came (hacia) _____ me, and I was afraid.
13. Henry is going with me (hasta) _____ New York.
14. Good-bye (hasta) _____ Tuesday.
15. Please don't turn on the light (de arriba de) _____ my bed.
16. John put his hat (encima de) _____ the letter.
17. I'm going to wash the wall (debajo de) _____ the window.
18. My book is (debajo de) _____ yours.
19. She lives two floors (abajo de) _____ him.
20. I'm going to put my book (debajo de) _____ yours.
21. Helen walked with them (hasta) _____ the store.
22. The wall (arriba de) _____ that chair is dirty.
23. We live (en) _____ 256 Water Street.
24. The water ran all (por) _____ the floor on Friday afternoon.
25. She said there was a man (debajo de) _____ her bed.

EXERCISE 6
Práctica verbal

1. We invite her.
2. We don't invite her.
3. Do we invite her?
4. Don't we invite her?
5. Why don't we invite her?
6. We invited you.
7. We didn't invite you.
8. Did we invite you?
9. Didn't we invite you?
10. Why didn't we invite you?
11. We're inviting them.
12. We aren't inviting them.
13. Are we inviting them?
14. Aren't we inviting them?
15. Why are we inviting them?
16. We were going to invite him.
17. We weren't going to invite him.
18. Were we going to invite him?
19. Weren't we going to invite him?
20. Why weren't we going to invite him?
21. We can invite the girls.
22. We can't invite the girls.
23. Can we invite the girls?
24. Can't we invite the girls?
25. Why can't we invite the girls?
26. We like to invite Mary.
27. We don't like to invite Mary.
28. Do we like to invite Mary?
29. Don't we like to invite Mary?
30. When do we like to invite Mary?
31. We have to invite Bob (Beto).
32. We don't have to invite Bob.
33. Do we have to invite Bob?
34. Don't we have to invite Bob?
35. Why do we have to invite Bob?

EXERCISE 7

Práctica verbal. *Repita el ejercicio 6, usando formas de los verbos* **meet, set, set the table, reply, hear, get to, get here (there), say good-bye (to)** *en oraciones cortas. Emplee un sustantivo o un pronombre distinto con cada verbo. Use las palabras interrogativas* **where** *y* **when** *cuando sea posible.*

EXERCISE 8

Lea y traduzca.

The fox and the stork

One day a fox met his friend, the stork. After they talked for a few minutes, the fox asked the stork if she could come to his house on Sunday.

"Certainly", replied the stork. "I can get there before twelve o'clock".

"Good", said the fox. "I'm going to invite you to have dinner with me".

On Sunday morning the stork went to the fox's house. When she got there, the fox was setting the table.

"Come in", said the fox, "and sit down. Dinner is almost ready. We're going to eat in a few minutes".

The fox put some flowers in a vase and set the vase on the table. Then he put two shallow plates on the table; and beside each plate he put a knife, a fork, and a spoon.

"Now", said the fox, "put your chair close to the table. It's time to eat, and dinner is ready. I'm going to bring the soup from the kitchen".

The fox went into the kitchen and came back with the soup. He put some soup in each plate and began to eat.

The stork couldn't drink the soup from the shallow plate with her long bill, so she was hungry all afternoon.

When the stork said good-bye to the fox, the fox said, "You didn't eat very much. I'm sorry that you didn't like the soup".

"That's all right", answered the stork. "It doesn't matter. It was a very interesting day, and I want you to come to my house next Sunday afternoon and have dinner with me".

The next Sunday the fox got to the stork's house at twelve o'clock. When the stork opened the door, she said, "Come in and sit down at the table. Dinner is ready".

Then she set two tall, narrow glasses on the table, put some soup in each glass, and set one of the glasses in front of the fox.

The stork put her long bill in the tall glass and drank and drank, but the fox couldn't put his big mouth in the narrow glass, so he was hungry all afternoon.

When the fox said good-bye, the stork said, "I see that you ate very little soup. Do you want to hear that I'm sorry (cuánto lo siento)?".

EXERCISE 9
Escriba en inglés.

1. Llegué antes que usted.
2. Por supuesto, este libro es mío.
3. Lo conocí a él en Acapulco el año pasado.
4. ¿Por qué no me dijo que iba a Estados Unidos dentro de (in) unos pocos días?
5. Había poca gente en la calle ayer.
6. ¿No quieres comer un poco?
7. No llevemos mucho dinero con nosotros.
8. Claro que no importa si él regresa.
9. Cuando llegamos a la puerta, él dijo –Pase.
10. Que yo sepa, él no estaba usando el teléfono.

EXERCISE 10
Dictado

1. Mother is setting the table for breakfast. It's time to eat.
2. We got to school at eight-thirty, but we were late.
3. Did you meet her in Taxco last week?
4. Don't put that spoon in your mouth because it's dirty.
5. Let's not go to the movies tonight. Let's read this interesting book.
6. If he doesn't have too much to do, let him help us.
7. Stand up. I want to see if your dress is too long.
8. Mary doesn't like to live on this narrow street.
9. If you get home on Saturday, come to see me in the afternoon.
10. I know you can't bring the book on Wednesday, but that's all right.

EXERCISE 11
Conversación. *Conteste las siguientes preguntas.*

1. When is your saint's day?
2. When is your birthday?
3. What time is it?
4. How old are you?
5. Where do you live?
6. Who set the table?
7. What time did you get to the office?
8. What time did you get home?
9. When did you get here?
10. When can you get there?

Conteste las siguientes preguntas en el afirmativo y en el negativo.

11. Are there many teachers in the school?
12. Is there always money in the house?
13. Is there water in the glass?
14. Do you ever go to the movies on Monday?
15. Do you ever visit Mary on Sunday?
16. Do you ever get up at six o'clock?
17. Do you ever get to the office early?
18. Do you often go to the movies on Saturday?
19. Do you usually go to the movies on Sunday?
20. Did he reply in English?
21. Did she set the glasses on the table?
22. Did she invite you to eat with her?
23. Did he meet you at the movies?
24. Did he get there at twenty minutes after nine?
25. Did they watch TV a lot?

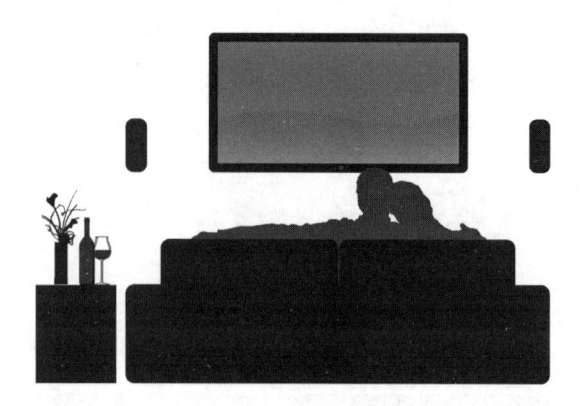

Lesson 18

VOCABULARY

1. **to lose, lost** perder, perdió
2. **to win, won** ganar, ganó (*de jugar*)
3. **to start, started** empezar, empezó
4. **to close, closed** cerrar, cerró
5. **to stop, stopped** detenerse, se detuvo
6. **to listen (to), listened (to)** escuchar, escuchó
7. **rabbit** conejo
8. **turtle** tortuga
9. **animal** animal
10. **race** carrera; raza
11. **grass** pasto; hierba
12. **tree** árbol
13. **eye** ojo
14. **cup** taza
15. **saucer** plato (*de taza*)
16. **cake** pastel
17. **coffee** café (*bebida*)
18. **apple** manzana

IDIOMS

1. **to go to sleep** dormirse; irse a dormir
2. **to go to bed** acostarse, irse a la cama
3. **to get sleepy** entrarle a uno sueño, darle a uno sueño
4. **after a while** después de un rato
5. **What color is it?** ¿De qué color es?
   It's blue. Es azul.
6. **He went out of town.** Él salió de la ciudad.
   He's out of town. Él está fuera de la ciudad.

He was out of town. Él estaba fuera de la ciudad.
7. **He started home.** Él salió para su casa.
8. **I listened to the radio.** Oí el radio.

EXERCISE 1
Traduzca las siguientes oraciones y practique leyéndolas.

1. Jump over him (bríncalo).
2. Don't jump over him.
3. Let's jump over it.
4. Let's not jump over it.
5. Let him jump over the fence.
6. Don't let him jump over the fence.
7. Let them jump over me.
8. Don't let them jump over me.
9. Those men hear you.
10. Those men don't hear you.
11. Do those men hear you?
12. Don't those men hear you?
13. These women met me yesterday.
14. These women didn't meet me yesterday.
15. Did these women meet me yesterday?
16. Didn't these women meet me yesterday?
17. That girl is going to lie down.
18. That girl isn't going to lie down.
19. Is that girl going to lie down?
20. Isn't that girl going to lie down?

Los pronombres y adjetivos indefinidos
some, any, no, none

some	algún; alguno(s)	**no**	no; ningún
any	algún; alguno(s)	**none**	ninguno
not... any	no; ninguno; ningún		

El empleo de estas palabras en inglés es en varias ocasiones idiomático, y por lo tanto muchas veces no se puede traducir. Es preciso siempre tener presente, tanto en el estudio de estas palabras como en las siguientes, que el inglés no permite doble negación.

Some

Se emplea la palabra **some** como adjetivo, o como pronombre cuando el verbo y el sentido de la oración son afirmativos. Como adjetivo, **some** siempre va acompañado de sustantivo, y como pronombre, siempre se refiere a algo ya mencionado o sobreentendido. Estudie las siguientes oraciones:

(verbo afirmativo y sentido afirmativo)	1. He has **some** books.	Él tiene algunos libros.
(verbo afirmativo y sentido afirmativo)	2. He has **some**.	Él tiene algunos.
(verbo afirmativo y sentido afirmativo)	3. He wants **some** coffee.	Él quiere café.
(verbo afirmativo y sentido afirmativo)	4. He wants **some**.	Él quiere.
(verbo afirmativo y sentido afirmativo)	5. **Some** of the boys came.	Algunos de los muchachos vinieron.

Any, not... any

Se emplea la palabra **any** como adjetivo o pronombre cuando el verbo está en negativo o cuando la oración está en interrogativo. Como adjetivo, **any** siempre va acompañado de un sustantivo, y como pronombre, siempre se refiere a algo ya mencionado o sobreentendido.

Acuérdese usted de que el inglés no permite doble negación y fíjese en las traducciones de los ejemplos.

(verbo negativo)	1. He doesn't have **any** book.	Él no tiene ningún libro.
(verbo negativo)	2. He doesn't have **any**.	Él no tiene ninguno.
(verbo negativo)	3. He doesn't want **any** coffee.	El no quiere café.
(verbo negativo)	4. He doesn't want **any**.	Él no quiere (café).
(oración interrogativa)	5. Does he have **any** books?	¿Tiene algunos libros?
(oración interrogativa)	6. Does he have **any**?	¿Tiene algunos?
(oración interrogativa negativa)	7. Doesn't he want **any** coffee?	¿No quiere café?
(oración interrogativa negativa)	8. Doesn't he want **any**?	¿No quiere?

EXERCISE 2

Llene los espacios con **any** *o* **some** *y traduzca.*

1. Is there _____ bread in the kitchen?
2. Yes, there's _____ bread in the kitchen.
3. No, there isn't _____ bread in the kitchen.
4. I'm going to buy _____ for dinner.
5. Do you see _____ people on the street?
6. Yes, I see _____.
7. No, I don't see _____.
8. Did they give you _____ money?
9. No, they didn't give me _____ money.
10. Yes, they gave us _____.

No, none

Se emplean las palabras **no** y **none** cuando el verbo está en afirmativo, pero el sentido de la oración es negativo. Dado que **no** es un adjetivo, siempre irá acompañado de un sustantivo; y puesto que **none** es un pronombre, no llevará ningún sustantivo, sino que se referirá a algo ya mencionado o sobreentendido. Las palabras **no** y **none** equivalen a **not... any**; la correlación **not... any** es mucho más usual.

Recuerde usted que el inglés no permite doble negación y fíjese en las traducciones de los ejemplos.

(verbo afirmativo y sentido negativo)	1. He has **no** book. (He does**n't** have **any** book.)	Él no tiene ningún libro.
(verbo afirmativo y sentido negativo)	2. He has **none**. (He does**n't** have **any**.)	Él no tiene ninguno.
(verbo afirmativo y sentido negativo)	3. He wants **no** coffee. (He does**n't** want **any** coffee.)	Él no quiere café.
(verbo afirmativo y sentido negativo)	4. He wants **none**. (He does**n't** want **any**.)	Él no quiere (café).
(verbo afirmativo y sentido negativo)	5. **None** of the boys came.	Ninguno de los muchachos vino.

EXERCISE 3

*Llene los espacios con **no** o **none** y traduzca.*

1. He says he has _____ book.
2. Did he say he has _____?
3. No, he says he has _____.
4. Did he say he had _____ pencil?
5. No, he said he had _____ book.
6. We have _____ books.
7. How much money do you have? I have _____.
8. How much money do you have? I have _____ money.
9. How much time do you have? I have _____.
10. How much time do you have? I have _____ time.

EXERCISE 4

*Llene los espacios con **any, some, no, none** y traduzca.*

1. Did you see _____ Americans?
2. No, I didn't see _____.
3. I saw _____ in Acapulco. (*afirmativo*)
4. Didn't you see _____ in the Hotel del Prado?
5. No, I didn't see _____ in the Hotel del Prado, but I saw _____ on the street.
6. I saw _____ Americans. (*negativo*)
7. No, I saw _____.
8. Do you have _____ children?
9. No, we have _____.
10. No, we have _____ children.
11. Yes, we have _____ children.
12. No, we don't have _____ children, but they have _____.

LESSON 18

13. They have _____ children (*afirmativo*), but we have _____.
14. We have _____ children (*negativo*), but they have _____.
15. We don't have _____, but they have _____.
16. Does John have _____ brothers?
17. No, he doesn't have _____ brothers, but I have _____.
18. No, John has _____ brothers, but he has _____ sisters.
19. Do you have _____ sisters?
20. Yes, I have _____ sisters, but _____ brothers.
21. No, I don't have _____ brothers, but I have _____ sisters.
22. No, I have _____ brothers.
23. No, I have _____.
24. I have _____ brothers. (*afirmativo*)
25. Yes, I have _____.

Something, anything, not... anything, nothing

something	algo, alguna cosa
anything	algo, alguna cosa
not... anything	nada, ninguna cosa
nothing	nada, ninguna cosa

La regla para el empleo de las siguientes palabras es igual a la que hemos visto anteriormente.

Se emplea **something** cuando el verbo y el sentido de la oración están en afirmativo. Se emplea **anything** cuando la oración tiene un verbo en negativo o cuando la oración es interrogativa.

LESSON 18

Se emplea **nothing** cuando el verbo es afirmativo pero el sentido de la oración es negativo. **Not... anything** equivale a **nothing**; aquél es mucho más usual.

Recuerde usted que el inglés no permite doble negación y fíjese en las traducciones de los ejemplos.

(verbo afirmativo y sentido afirmativo)	1. He wants **something**.	Él quiere algo.
(verbo afirmativo y sentido afirmativo)	2. **Something** happened.	Algo pasó.
(verbo negativo)	3. He doesn't want **anything**.	No quiere nada.
(verbo afirmativo y sentido negativo)	4. He wants **nothing**.	No quiere nada.
(verbo afirmativo y sentido negativo)	5. **Nothing** happened.	No pasó nada. (Nada pasó.)
(oración interrogativa)	6. Does he want **anything**?	¿Quiere algo?
(oración interrogativa negativa)	7. Doesn't he want **anything**?	¿No quiere nada (algo)?

EXERCISE 5

Llene los espacios con **anything, something, nothing** *y traduzca.*

1. They don't have _____.
2. They don't have _____, but I have _____.
3. We have _____. (*negativo*)

4. She has _____ to do. (*negativo*)
5. Don't you have _____ to do?
6. No, I don't have _____ to do.
7. I have _____ to do. (*negativo*)
8. I have _____ to do. (*afirmativo*)
9. Did he buy _____ in New York?
10. Yes, he bought _____ in New York.
11. No, he didn't buy _____ in New York.
12. No, he bought _____ in New York.
13. Did she see _____ under the bed?
14. Yes, she saw _____ under the bed.
15. No, she didn't see _____ under the bed.
16. No, she saw _____ under the bed.
17. Did you put _____ in your coffee?
18. Yes, I put _____ in my coffee.
19. No, I didn't put _____ in my coffee.
20. No, I put _____ in my coffee.
21. Did you hear _____?
22. No, I didn't hear _____.
23. He said he heard _____. (*afirmativo*)
24. I don't think he heard _____.
25. He said he heard _____. (*negativo*)
26. Did you have _____ to eat this morning?
27. No, we didn't have _____ to eat this morning, but we had _____ to eat last night.
28. We had _____ to eat this morning. (*negativo*)
29. We had _____ to eat last night. (*afirmativo*)
30. Did she tell you _____?
31. Did she say _____ to you?
32. Yes, she said _____ to me.
33. No, she didn't say _____ to me.
34. No, she said _____ to me.
35. Didn't she say _____ to you?

Somebody (someone), anybody (anyone), not... anybody (anyone), nobody (no one)

somebody (someone)	alguien, alguna persona
anybody (anyone)	alguien, alguna persona
not... anybody (anyone)	nadie, ninguna persona
nobody (no one)	nadie, ninguna persona

La regla para el empleo de las siguientes palabras es igual a la que hemos visto anteriormente.

Se emplea **somebody (someone)** cuando el verbo y el sentido de la oración están en afirmativo. Se emplea **anybody (anyone)** cuando la oración tiene un verbo en negativo o cuando la oración es interrogativa.

Se emplea **nobody (no one)** cuando el verbo está en afirmativo, pero el sentido de la oración es negativo. **Not... anybody (anyone)** equivale a **nobody (no one)**; aquellos son mucho más usuales.

Recuerde usted que el inglés no permite doble negación y fíjese en las traducciones de los ejemplos.

(verbo afirmativo y sentido afirmativo)	1. He saw **somebody**.	Él vio a alguien.
(verbo afirmativo y sentido afirmativo)	2. **Someone** called.	Alguien llamó.
(verbo negativo)	3. He did**n't** see **anybody**.	No vio a nadie.
(verbo afirmativo y sentido negativo)	4. He saw **nobody**.	No vio a nadie.
(verbo afirmativo y sentido negativo)	5. **No one** came.	Nadie vino. (No vino nadie.)
(oración interrogativa)	6. Did he see **anybody**?	¿Vio él a alguien?

(oración interrogativa)	7. Did**n't** he see **anyone**?	¿No vio él a nadie (a alguien)?
(verbo afirmativo y sentido afirmativo)	8. **Somebody** said **something**.	Alguien dijo algo.
(verbo afirmativo y sentido negativo)	9. **Nobody** said **anything**.	Nadie dijo nada.

EXERCISE 6

Llene los espacios con **anybody (anyone)**, **somebody (someone)**, **nobody (no one)** *y traduzca.*

1. Did _____ come this afternoon?
2. Yes, _____ came this afternoon.
3. No, _____ came this afternoon.
4. I didn't see _____.
5. _____ was there. (*negativo*)
6. _____ was there. (*afirmativo*)
7. Wasn't _____ there?
8. No, _____ was there.
9. Don't tell _____.
10. No, I'm not going to tell _____.
11. Did you tell _____?
12. No, I told _____.
13. No, I didn't tell _____.
14. You can ask _____.
15. You can't ask _____.
16. Can't you ask _____?
17. Don't ask _____.
18. He's going to visit _____.
19. Is he going to visit _____?
20. No, he isn't going to visit _____.
21. No, he's going to visit _____.

22. We see _____ in the garden. (*negativo*)
23. We don't see _____ in the garden.
24. We see _____ in the garden. (*afirmativo*)
25. Can't we see _____ in the garden?
26. Yes, we can see _____ in the garden.
27. They didn't talk to _____.
28. They talked to _____. (*negativo*)
29. Did they talk to _____?
30. No, they didn't talk to _____.
31. Why didn't they talk to _____?
32. Do you know _____ in Monterrey?
33. Yes, I know _____ there.
34. No, I know _____ in Monterrey.
35. No, I don't know _____ in Monterrey.

Somewhere (some place), anywhere (any place), not... anywhere (any place), nowhere (no place)

somewhere (some place)	alguna parte, algún lado
anywhere (any place)	alguna parte, algún lado
not... anywhere (any place)	ninguna parte, ningún lado
nowhere (no place)	ninguna parte, ningún lado

La regla para el empleo de las siguientes palabras es igual a la que hemos visto anteriormente.

Se emplea **somewhere (some place)** cuando el verbo y el sentido de la oración están en afirmativo. Se emplea **anywhere (any place)** cuando la oración tiene el verbo en negativo o cuando la oración es interrogativa.

Se emplea **nowhere (no place)** cuando el verbo está en afirmativo pero el sentido de la oración es negativo. **Not... anywhere (any place)** equivalen a **nowhere (no place)**; aquéllos son mucho más usuales.

Recuerde usted que el inglés no permite doble negación y fíjese en las traducciones de los ejemplos.

(verbo afirmativo y sentido afirmativo)	1. He went **some place**.	Él fue a alguna parte.
(verbo negativo)	2. He did**n't** go **anywhere**.	Él no fue a ningún lado.
(verbo afirmativo y sentido negativo)	3. He went **nowhere**.	Él no fue a ningún lado.
(oración interrogativa)	4. Did he go **anywhere**?	¿Fue él a alguna parte?
(oración interrogativa)	5. Didn't he go **anywhere**?	¿No fue él a ninguna (a alguna) parte?
(verbo afirmativo y sentido afirmativo)	6. **Somebody** went **some place**.	Alguien fue a alguna parte.
(verbo afirmativo y sentido negativo)	7. **Nobody** went **anywhere**.	Nadie fue a ningún lado.

EXERCISE 7

Llene los espacios con **anywhere (any place)**, **somewhere (some place)**, **nowhere (no place)** *y traduzca.*

1. Are you going _____?
2. Yes, I'm going _____.
3. No, I'm not going _____.
4. No, I'm going _____.
5. He took her _____ yesterday. (*afirmativo*)
6. Did he take her _____ yesterday?
7. No, he didn't take her _____ yesterday.

8. No, he never takes her _____.
9. Why doesn't he ever take her _____?
10. Take her _____. (*afirmativo*)
11. Don't take her_____.
12. Never take her _____.
13. He's going to put it _____.
14. He isn't going to put it _____.
15. Is he going to put it _____?
16. Isn't he going to put it _____?
17. Let him go _____ with her.
18. Don't let him go _____ with her.
19. Let's go _____ tonight.
20. Let's not go _____ tonight.
21. Nobody went _____ last night.
22. Bob went _____ last night.
23. Did you go _____ last night?
24. Why didn't you go _____ on Sunday?
25. I didn't go _____ on Sunday, but I went _____ on Saturday.

Everything, everybody (everyone) everywhere (every place)

everything	todo, todas las cosas
everybody (everyone)	todos, todo el mundo
everywhere (every place)	por, a, en todas partes

Se emplean las palabras **everything, everybody (everyone), everywhere (every place)** en oraciones afirmativas, negativas, interrogativas o interrogativas negativas.

Las palabras **everybody (everyone), everything** siempre llevan el verbo en singular. Estudie las siguientes oraciones.

(afirmativo)	1. He has **everything**.	Él tiene todo.
(afirmativo)	2. **Everybody** is sick.	Todo el mundo está mal (enfermo).
(interrogativo)	3. Is **everyone** here?	¿Están todos aquí?
(interrogativo negativo)	4. Isn't **everyone** here?	¿No están todos aquí?
(negativo)	5. He didn't look **everywhere**.	Él no buscó por todas partes.
(interrogativo)	6. Did he look **everywhere**?	¿Buscó él por todas partes?

EXERCISE 8

Llene los espacios, con **everything, everybody (everyone), everywhere (every place)**, *y traduzca.*

1. Do you have (todo) _____?
2. Is (todos) _____ here?
3. (Todo el mundo) _____ wants to go.
4. Did you look (por todas partes) _____?
5. We looked for the children (por todos lados) _____.
6. Did you eat (todo) _____?
7. Is (todos) _____ listening to me?
8. There are grass and trees (por todos lados) _____.
9. My father does (todo) _____.
10. Let's invite (todo el mundo) _____.
11. (Todos) _____ is sick.
12. (Todo) _____ happens to him.
13. We saw John's parents (por todos sitios) _____.

LESSON 18

14. The teacher was mad at (todos) _____.
15. Is (todo) _____ ready?
16. (Por todos lados) _____ I look, I see them.
17. (A todos) _____ likes coffee and cake.
18. She sold (todo) _____ in her house.
19. They liked to go (a todas partes) _____.
20. (Todo el mundo) _____ is asking the same question.
21. He thinks that (todo) _____ is easy.
22. We were looking for you (por todas partes) _____.
23. How is (todos) _____?
24. He had friends (en todas partes) _____.
25. (Todo el mundo) _____ is doing something.

Verbos y preposiciones

Estudie los siguientes verbos y preposiciones.

1. **to go out** salir
   He went out. Él salió.
2. **to go out of** salir de
   He went out of the room. Él salió del cuarto.
3. **to look out** asomarse
   He looked out. Él se asomó.
4. **to look out of** asomarse por
   He looked out of the window. Él se asomó por la ventana.
5. **to take (something) out** sacar (algo)
   He took the flowers out. Sacó las flores.
6. **to take (something) out of** sacar (algo) de
   He took the flowers out of the vase. Sacó las flores del florero.
7. **out of** fuera de
8. **outside** afuera (*de un local*), fuera de
9. **up** arriba, hacia arriba
10. **down** abajo, hacia abajo

EXERCISE 9
Traduzca las siguientes oraciones. Cámbielas al negativo, interrogativo e interrogativo negativo.

1. He goes out of town every Sunday.
2. He went out of town last week.
3. They go out about nine o'clock.
4. They went out yesterday for an hour.
5. She can look out of the window.
6. She looked out of the door.
7. She's looking out of the window.
8. She was going to look out of the window.
9. You took something out.
10. He took the flowers out of the vase.
11. He was taking the bed out of the bedroom.
12. He's going to take the chair out of the living room.

EXERCISE 10
Llene los espacios con la preposición correcta y traduzca.

1. My husband went (salió de) _____ town yesterday.
2. Do you want to go (salir de) _____ town on your saint's day?
3. He was walking (calle abajo) _____ the street when I saw him.
4. I looked (hacia abajo) _____, but I didn't see anything.
5. He looked (hacia arriba) _____, but he didn't see anybody.
6. Don't look (hacia arriba) _____; look (hacia abajo) _____.
7. Why don't you go (sales de) _____ town next week?
8. They're (fuera de) _____ the city.
9. Tell the child to wait (afuera) _____.
10. The man is waiting (afuera) _____.
11. Come (bájate) _____ from that tree.

12. She was very tired when she came (subió) _____.
13. She looked (se asomó) _____, but she didn't see anything.
14. You can see the school from here if you look (se asoma por) _____ that window.
15. Why did you look (te asomaste) _____?
16. I want to sleep, so please take the children (saca)_____
17. I'm going to take the glasses (sacar de) _____ the dining room and wash them.
18. How many did you take (sacó) _____?
19. She took the bread (sacó de) _____ the kitchen.
20. I want to take that rug (sacar de) _____ the house.
21. She was sick yesterday and couldn't go (salir de) _____ her room.
22. I went (salí) _____ with a very nice girl last night.
23. Are you going to go (salir) _____ with her tonight?
24. I can see them if I look (me asomo por) _____ the door.
25. Why are you taking your dresses (sacando) _____?
26. If you aren't feeling well, don't go (salgas) _____.
27. Don't be afraid to look (asomarse por) _____ the window.
28. Don't take that chair (saque de) _____ the living room.

EXERCISE 11
Práctica verbal

1. He always loses them.
2. He doesn't always lose them.
3. Does he always lose them?
4. Doesn't he always lose them?
5. Why does he always lose them?
6. He lost it at school.
7. He didn't lose it at school.

8. Did he lose it at school?
9. Didn't he lose it at school?
10. How did he lose it at school?
11. He's going to lose everything.
12. He isn't going to lose everything.
13. Is he going to lose everything?
14. Isn't he going to lose everything?
15. How is he going to lose everything?
16. He was losing the race.
17. He wasn't losing the race.
18. Was he losing the race?
19. Wasn't he losing the race?
20. Why was he losing the race?
21. He wanted to lose both.
22. He didn't want to lose both.
23. Did he want to lose both?
24. Didn't he want to lose both?
25. Why did he want to lose both?
26. He could lose this one.
27. He couldn't lose this one.
28. Could he lose this one?
29. Couldn't he lose this one?
30. Why couldn't he lose this one?
31. He had to lose it.
32. He didn't have to lose it.
33. Did he have to lose it?
34. Didn't he have to lose it?
35. Why did he have to lose it?

EXERCISE 12

Práctica verbal. *Repita el ejercicio 11, usando formas de los verbos* **win, start, close, go to sleep, go to bed, stop, listen (to), get sleepy** *en oraciones cortas. Emplee un sustantivo o pronombre distinto con cada verbo. Use las palabras interrogativas* **how** *y* **why** *cuando sea posible.*

EXERCISE 13
Lea y traduzca.

The rabbit and the turtle

A rabbit was always laughing at a turtle because he couldn't run very fast. The turtle never got mad at the rabbit when the rabbit laughed at him. One day the rabbit said to the turtle, "All the animals here know that you can run very fast, so let's run a race".

All the other animals began to laugh at the turtle because they knew that he was very slow, and they thought he was afraid to run a race with the rabbit.

Then the turtle began to get angry. "I'm tired of everyone saying that I'm slow", he said, "and if the rabbit wants to run a race, I'm ready".

"You can start here", said the fox, and run as far as that big tree over there in the next field. "We're going to be there to meet the one who finishes the race first".

"O.K.", said the turtle. "Let's start the race".

The rabbit started to run very fast, and soon he was so far from the turtle that he couldn't see him.

"I'm going to stop for a few minutes and wait until the turtle gets here", said the rabbit. So he sat down on the grass under a big tree.

After a while he began to get sleepy; so he lay down on the grass, closed his eyes, and went to sleep.

Sometime later the turtle, going very slowly, passed by the tree and saw the rabbit asleep under it. The rabbit slept and slept. When he woke up, he saw all the animals under the big tree in the field, and he heard the fox telling the other animals that the turtle won the race.

The rabbit ran to the tree, but of course he got there too late. The fox said to him, "You lost the race and the turtle won it".

EXERCISE 14

Escriba en inglés. Use las palabras **some** *y* **any** *siempre que sea posible.*

1. ¿Encontraste a alguien en la calle?
2. No, no encontré a nadie.
3. Él me dijo que tenía (algunas) manzanas.
4. ¿Les diste a ellos café?
5. No, no les di café.
6. ¿Dónde están todos?
7. María tiene algo para usted, pero nada para mí.
8. Llegaremos a México el 13 de septiembre.
9. Si camina usted hacia la casa, puede ver la luz en la sala.
10. Hoy no tengo nada que hacer, porque lo hice todo ayer.
11. Nadie comió nada.
12. Todos van a ir a alguna parte.

EXERCISE 15
Dictado

1. His birthday is on the 31st of August, and his saint's day is on the 5th of July.
2. Nobody came to visit me on Sunday.
3. Everybody likes my new blue suit.
4. There wasn't any coffee, so my mother went into the kitchen to make some.
5. Do you ever get sleepy before ten o'clock?
6. I went to bed very early last night, but I didn't go to sleep until eleven-thirty.
7. Don't you see those animals coming toward you?
8. I listened to the radio last night, but after a while I got sleepy.
9. We stopped in front of your house last night and saw you looking out of the window.
10. I'm sorry, but you can't talk to Mr. Carter. He's out of town.

EXERCISE 16
Conversación. *Conteste las siguientes preguntas.*

1. What color are your eyes?
2. What color is your dress?
3. What color is your book?

Conteste las siguientes preguntas en afirmativo y en negativo.

4. Did you listen to the radio last night?
5. Did you start home at four-fifteen?
6. Did she go any place last night?
7. Aren't you going anywhere tomorrow?
8. Did you go anywhere last Sunday?
9. Did you look everywhere?
10. Do you ever go any place at night?
11. Don't you ever go anywhere?
12. Do you ever watch TV?
13. Do you have anything to eat?
14. Does he have anything to do?
15. Does she have anything to read?
16. Do you see anybody?
17. Did he buy any?
18. Did she sell any dresses?
19. Did you leave anything on the table?
20. Did she say anything?
21. Did you lose anything?
22. Did you hear anyone?
23. Did he ask anyone?
24. Did she tell anybody?
25. Did you go out of town last week?

Lesson 19

VOCABULARY

1. **to show, showed** mostrar, mostró, enseñar, enseñó
2. **to hurry, hurried** apresurarse, se apresuró
3. **to kill, killed** matar, mató
4. **to cut, cut** cortar, cortó
5. **to become, became** llegar a ser, llegó a ser; hacerse, se hizo; volverse, se volvió; ponerse, se puso
6. **to love, loved** amar, amó
7. **as** mientras; cuando
8. **while** mientras que
9. **once** una vez
10. **again** otra vez
11. **busy** ocupado
12. **rich** rico
13. **poor** pobre
14. **pure** puro
15. **beautiful** hermoso, guapa
16. **gold** oro, de oro
    golden de oro; dorado
17. **goose** gansa, oca
    geese gansos, ocas
18. **farm** granja
    farmer granjero
19. **food** alimento, comida
20. **another** otro
21. **hand** mano

IDIOMS

1. **to lay eggs, laid eggs** poner huevos, puso huevos
2. **to get rich, got rich** hacerse rico, se hizo rico
3. **at once** inmediatamente; de una vez
4. **Hurry (up).** Apresúrese.

5. **I'm in a hurry.** Estoy de prisa. Tengo prisa.
6. **scrambled eggs** huevos revueltos
   fried eggs huevos fritos
   boiled eggs huevos cocidos
7. **to be about** tratar de
   What's the book about? ¿De qué trata el libro?
   What's it about? ¿De qué trata?
   It's about animals. Trata de animales.
8. **not... either** no... tampoco
   I didn't go either. Yo no fui tampoco, Tampoco fui yo.

EXERCISE 1
Traduzca las siguientes oraciones y practique leyéndolas.

1. Let them win.
2. Don't let them win.
3. What's the story about?
4. The story is about a farmer.
5. The story isn't about a farmer.
6. Is the story about a farmer?
7. Isn't the story about a farmer?
8. What was it about?
9. It was about a poor farmer.
10. It wasn't about a poor farmer.
11. Was it about a poor farmer?
12. Wasn't it about a poor farmer?
13. That goose laid an egg yesterday.
14. That goose didn't lay an egg yesterday.
15. Did that goose lay an egg yesterday?
16. Didn't that goose lay an egg yesterday?
17. He's listening to the radio.
18. He isn't listening to the radio.
19. Is he listening to the radio?
20. Isn't he listening to the radio?

El equivalente de ¿no es verdad?

Para traducir las preguntas **¿no es verdad?**, **¿verdad?**, **¿no?**, **¿no es así?**, con las que se pide asentimiento o confirmación, se repite el pronombre (o el pronombre correspondiente al sustantivo) y se usa el auxiliar que se emplearía para poner el verbo en negativo.

Si el primer verbo de la oración es afirmativo, el auxiliar en la pregunta corta estará en negativo. Si el primer verbo es negativo, el auxiliar en la pregunta corta estará en afirmativo. Estudie los siguientes ejemplos.

1. It's clean, **isn't it?**
   It isn't clean, **is it?**
2. There's time, **isn't there?**
   There isn't any time, **is there?**
3. He's eating, **isn't he?**
   He isn't eating, **is he?**
4. They're going to come, **aren't they?**
   They aren't going to come, **are they?**
5. You were writing, **weren't you?**
   You weren't writing, **were you?**
6. I have to eat, **don't I?**
   I don't have to eat, **do I?**
7. The car works, **doesn't it?**
   The car doesn't work, **does it?**
8. Henry likes to teach, **doesn't he?**
   Henry doesn't like to teach, **does he?**
9. John's sister went, **didn't she?**
   John's sister didn't go, **did she?**
10. Your brother wanted to sleep, **didn't he?**
    Your brother didn't want to sleep, **did he?**
11. John can win, **can't he?**
    John can't win, **can he?**
12. Mary and I could study, **couldn't we?**
    Mary and I couldn't study, **could we?**

EXERCISE 2
Traduzca las siguientes oraciones.

1. Tú trabajas en una tienda, ¿verdad?
2. No trabajas en una tienda, ¿verdad?
3. Trabajaste en una tienda, ¿verdad?
4. No trabajaste en una tienda, ¿verdad?
5. Él va a traer el dinero, ¿verdad?
6. Él no va a traer el dinero, ¿verdad?
7. Él iba a traer el dinero, ¿verdad?
8. Él no iba a traer el dinero, ¿verdad?
9. Ella está regresando, ¿verdad?
10. Ella no está regresando, ¿verdad?
11. Ella estaba regresando, ¿verdad?
12. Ella no estaba regresando, ¿verdad?
13. Podemos olvidar, ¿verdad?
14. No podemos olvidar, ¿verdad?
15. Pudimos olvidar, ¿verdad?
16. No pudimos olvidar, ¿verdad?
17. A ustedes les gusta oír el radio, ¿verdad?
18. A ustedes no les gusta oír el radio, ¿verdad?
19. A ustedes les gustó oír el radio, ¿verdad?
20. A ustedes no les gustó oír el radio, ¿verdad?
21. Ellos quieren saber, ¿verdad?
22. Ellos no quieren saber, ¿verdad?
23. Ellos quisieron saber, ¿verdad?
24. Ellos no quisieron saber, ¿verdad?
25. Juan tiene que levantarse temprano, ¿verdad?
26. Juan no tiene que levantarse temprano, ¿verdad?
27. Juan tuvo que levantarse temprano, ¿verdad?
28. Juan no tuvo que levantarse temprano, ¿verdad?
29. María entiende el inglés, ¿verdad?
30. María no entiende el inglés, ¿verdad?
31. María entendió el inglés, ¿verdad?
32. María no entendió el inglés, ¿verdad?

33. Las muchachas se ponen sus vestidos, ¿verdad?
34. Las muchachas no se ponen sus vestidos, ¿verdad?
35. Las muchachas se pusieron sus vestidos, ¿verdad?
36. Las muchachas no se pusieron sus vestidos, ¿verdad?
37. Puedo escribir, ¿verdad?
38. No puedo escribir, ¿verdad?
39. Pude escribir, ¿verdad?
40. No pude escribir, ¿verdad?
41. Alicia y yo ayudamos, ¿verdad?
42. Alicia y yo no ayudamos, ¿verdad?
43. Alicia y yo ayudábamos, ¿verdad?
44. Alicia y yo no ayudábamos, ¿verdad?
45. Usted y María se lavan, ¿verdad?
46. Usted Y María no se lavan, ¿verdad?
47. Usted y María se lavaron, ¿verdad?
48. Usted y María no se lavaron, ¿verdad?
49. Hay un libro, ¿verdad?
50. No hay un libro, ¿verdad?
51. Había dos muchachos, ¿verdad?
52. No había dos muchachos, ¿verdad?

EXERCISE 3

Llene los espacios con el equivalente correcto de **¿verdad?** *y traduzca.*

1. It doesn't make any difference, _____?
2. It's time to go, _____?
3. Walter doesn't have anything to do, _____?
4. It was Miss Stewart who turned on the TV, _____?
5. You were waiting for somebody, _____?
6. It's very late, _____?
7. There isn't any room, _____?
8. Mrs. Lane's little boy was seven years old the day before yesterday, _____?

9. That boy's name is Edward, _____?
10. It was very cold last night, _____?
11. You said good-bye to Mr. Burns, _____?
12. He couldn't come at five o'clock either, _____?
13. Sam didn't finish early, _____?
14. Dorothy's birthday is going to be the day after tomorrow, _____?
15. I can visit my grandmother every Thursday, _____?

To the teacher

Although prepositions will, normally, always govern the objective case, **whom** should not be used in conversational English as the object of a preposition that ends a sentence.

The tendency, when speaking English, is to use the nominative form **who** to introduce direct and indirect questions. Observe the following sentences.

> **Who** are you going to the movies with? (*direct*)
> **Who** have you been looking for? (*direct*)
> I asked him **who** he was talking to. (*indirect*)

Las preposiciones al final de la oración

Las preposiciones tales como **at, to, of, for, from, with, about** que se colocan al principio de las preguntas en español, en inglés van al final. Estudie las siguientes oraciones:

> 1. **What's** it made **of**? ¿De qué es?
> 2. **What** are you laughing **at**? ¿De qué te ríes?
> 3. **Who** are you going **with**? ¿Con quién vas?

4. **Where** did he come **from**? ¿De dónde vino él?
5. **What** are you looking **for**? ¿Qué busca usted?
6. **What** are they looking **at**? ¿Qué ven ellos?
7. **What** did you want that **for**? ¿Para qué quisiste eso?
8. **What** did he go home **for**? ¿Para qué fue él a casa?
He went home to eat. (*Recuérdese que no se usa la palabra* **for** *(para) antes de un infinitivo*). Pero: He went home **for** his book.
(*Se puede usar* **for** *antes de un sustantivo.*)
He went home **because** (*porque*) he was sick.

EXERCISE 4

Lea y traduzca las siguientes oraciones. Contéstelas, usando el vocabulario que ha visto con anterioridad.

1. Where are you from?
2. What city did you come from?
3. What country did your parents come from?
4. What state (estado) did your father come from?
5. What do you and your friend talk about?
6. What did you talk about?
7. What are you talking about?
8. What were you talking about?
9. What are you going to talk about?
10. What were you going to talk about?
11. What was the book about?
12. What was the movie about?
13. What was the lesson about?
14. What is the conversation about?
15. What are you laughing at?
16. What were you laughing at?

17. What are they looking at?
18. What were they looking at?
19. What is he listening to?
20. What was he listening to?
21. Who is she talking to?
22. Who was she talking to?
23. What are you thinking about?
24. What were you thinking of?
25. What are you looking for?
26. What was he looking for?
27. What are they going to look for?
28. What were they going to look for?
29. What are you working so hard for?
30. What are you taking that book for?
31. Who did he give that to?
32. What did you come so early for?
33. What did you give him the money for?
34. What did you say that for?
35. Who did she go with?
36. Who did he go to the movies with?
37. Who is he going with?
38. Who was he going with?
39. Who is he sitting with?
40. Who was he sitting with?
41. Who is he studying with?
42. Who is he living with?

EXERCISE 5
Traduzca estas oraciones, colocando la preposición al final de la pregunta.

1. ¿Para qué quieres eso?
2. ¿Para qué trajiste tu libro?
3. ¿Para qué lo vas a usar?

4. ¿A cuántos profesores vas a buscar?
5. ¿De dónde vino su esposa?
6. ¿De cuál escuela vinieron sus niños?
7. ¿De dónde vino toda esta agua?
8. ¿Con quién vino ella?
9. ¿Con quién fue ella?
10. ¿A quién dio él el dinero?
11. ¿De qué estaban hablando esos hombres?
12. ¿De qué trata la carta?
13. ¿En qué estás pensando?
14. ¿En qué estaban ellos pensando?
15. ¿De qué se está riendo esa muchacha?
16. ¿Qué estás buscando?
17. ¿Cuántos vas a buscar?
18. ¿Para qué necesitas el dinero?
19. ¿Para qué estás haciendo eso?
20. ¿Para qué estás llevando sombrero?

Preposiciones

Aprenda estas preposiciones.

1.	**through**	a través de, por
2.	**across**	al otro lado de
3.	**up to**	hasta
4.	**on the other side of**	más allá de, pasando, del otro lado de
5.	**between**	entre (refiriéndose a dos)
6.	**among**	entre (refiréndose a más de dos)

EXERCISE 6
Llene los espacios con la preposición correcta y traduzca.

1. The dog lay down (entre) _____ the trees.
2. The dog ran (entre) _____ the two boys.
3. The dog ran (a través de) _____ the house.
4. The dog ran (hasta) _____ the house.
5. We found the money (entre) _____ those two big chairs.
6. Isn't that man afraid to walk (entre) _____ all those animals?
7. If you walk (por) _____ the garden, you can see my beautiful flowers.
8. We went (por) _____ Chicago when we visited the United States.
9. She can work (hasta) _____ the 15th of August.
10. Texas is (al otro lado de) _____ the Rio Grande.
11. How many trees are there (entre) _____ my house and yours?
12. I think you can find your books (entre) _____ mine.
13. What are you walking (por) _____ my bedroom for?
14. The dining room is (entre) _____ the kitchen and the living room.
15. Did you ever live (entre) _____ Americans?
16. Taxco is (más allá de) _____ Cuernavaca.

EXERCISE 7
Llene los espacios con **any, some, no, none** *y traduzca.*

1. There's _____ milk in the house. (negativo)
2. That's why I couldn't drink _____ for breakfast.
3. I didn't drink _____ either.
4. Did you drink _____?
5. No, I didn't drink _____ because there was _____ in the house.
6. No, I drank _____ because there wasn't _____ in the house.
7. I am going to buy _____.
8. You can buy _____ at that store.
9. Yes, I think they have _____ in that store.
10. No, they have _____ milk in that store.

EXERCISE 8
Llene los espacios con **anything, something, nothing** *y traduzca.*

1. I'm going to the store. Do you want _____?
2. No, I don't want _____, but I think my mother wants _____.
3. She said she didn't want _____.
4. There's _____ (negativo) in the house to eat.
5. Buy _____ for dinner.
6. There's _____ (afirmativo) in the kitchen that we can eat.
7. No, there isn't _____ in the kitchen, and we have _____ (negativo) for dinner.
8. I didn't have _____ to eat for breakfast, but I'm going to have _____ to eat for dinner.
9. Don't you have _____ to do?
10. No, I have _____ to do.

LESSON 19

EXERCISE 9

Llene los espacios con **anybody (anyone)**, **somebody (someone)**, **nobody (no one)** *y traduzca.*

1. Did you talk to _____?
2. No, there was _____ to talk to?
3. Wasn't there _____ in the living room to talk to?
4. Yes, there was _____ in the living room to talk to, but _____ spoke English.
5. I'm going to invite _____ (afirmativo) that speaks English.
6. Don't invite _____ that can't speak English.
7. _____ (negativo) here can speak English.
8. Then find _____ that can speak English.
9. I know _____ (afirmativo) that can speak English.
10. I don't know _____ that can speak English.

EXERCISE 10

Llene los espacios con **anywhere (any place)**, **somewhere (some place)**, **nowhere (no place)** *y traduzca.*

1. I want to go _____ tomorrow.
2. I don't want to go _____ tomorrow.
3. Do you want to go _____ tomorrow?
4. No, I want to go _____ tomorrow.
5. Nobody wants to go _____ tomorrow.
6. They ate _____ near the office.
7. Did they eat _____ near the office?
8. No, they didn't eat _____ near the office.
9. They ate _____ close to the office.
10. They never like to eat _____ close to the office.

EXERCISE 11
Llene los espacios y traduzca.

1. He took (todo) _____.
2. (Todo el mundo) _____ knows him and likes him.
3. There are good and bad people (por todas partes) _____.
4. My parents always let me do (todo) _____.
5. Tell (todos) _____.
6. She taught (en todas partes) _____ in Mexico.
7. (Todo) _____ is going to be ready for tomorrow.
8. They woke up (todos) _____ in the house.
9. We're going to take them (a todos lados) _____.
10. (Todo el mundo) _____ is going to be hungry.

EXERCISE 12
Práctica verbal

1. He wants to become a doctor.
2. He doesn't want to become a doctor.
3. Does he want to become a doctor?
4. Doesn't he want to become a doctor?
5. When does he want to become a doctor?
6. He became a teacher.
7. He didn't become a teacher.
8. Did he become a teacher?
9. Didn't he become a teacher?
10. Why didn't he become a teacher?
11. He's going to become a farmer.
12. He isn't going to become a farmer.
13. Is he going to become a farmer?
14. Isn't he going to become a farmer?
15. When is he going to become a farmer?
16. He was going to become a doctor.

17. He wasn't going to become a doctor.
18. Was he going to become a doctor?
19. Wasn't he going to become a doctor?
20. Why wasn't he going to become a doctor?
21. He can become a teacher.
22. He can't become a teacher.
23. Can he become a teacher?
24. Can't he become a teacher?
25. Why can't he become a teacher?
26. He has to become a farmer.
27. He doesn't have to become a farmer.
28. Does he have to become a farmer?
29. Doesn't he have to become a farmer?
30. Why does he have to become a farmer?
31. He had to become a doctor.
32. He didn't have to become a doctor.
33. Did he have to become a doctor?
34. Didn't he have to become a doctor?
35. Why did he have to become a doctor?

EXERCISE 13
Práctica verbal. *Repita el ejercicio 12, usando formas de los verbos* **hurry, show, kill, get rich, cut, love, lay eggs** *en oraciones cortas. Emplee un sustantivo o pronombre distinto con cada verbo. Use las palabras interrogativas* **why** *y* **when** *cuando sea posible.*

EXERCISE 14
Lea y traduzca.

The goose that laid the golden egg

Once there was a farmer who lived with his wife on a farm in the country. They had to work hard every day because they were very poor. Often there wasn't any food in the house to eat.

The farmer and his wife had a cow and a goose. The cow gave milk, and the goose laid eggs. Every day the farmer went to the barn to get the egg that the goose laid. Sometimes there was no egg in the barn, so the farmer and his wife had to go to bed hungry.

One night when the farmer went to get the egg, he was very happy to find a goose egg of pure gold in the barn.

The farmer took the egg, hurried to the house, and showed it to his wife, saying, "Look. Our goose laid a golden egg. We're going to be rich".

"Let me see", said the farmer's wife. She put her hand on the egg and felt it. "It's gold-pure gold", she said. "Now we're never going to go to bed hungry again".

The next day the farmer found another beautiful golden egg in the barn. And the next day and the next the goose laid a golden egg, and the farmer and his wife got very rich. Now they didn't have to work, and there was always food in the house to eat.

As the farmer got rich, he began to think more and more of having all the golden eggs at once. One day he said to his wife, "Let's kill the goose that lays the golden eggs, and then we can have all the eggs at once. I want to be very rich".

"All right", answered his wife. "Go get (ve por) the goose".

The farmer brought the goose in the house and put her on the table.

Then, while his wife helped him, he killed the goose. He cut her open (le abrió) with a knife and found–nothing!

They killed the goose that laid the golden egg.

EXERCISE 15
Escriba en inglés.

1. Apresúrese. Estoy de prisa y no puedo esperar.
2. ¿Nunca puedes llegar temprano?
3. El granjero se hizo rico porque tenía una gansa que puso un huevo de oro.
4. ¿Por qué estabas caminando entre estos dos hombres?
5. Llevé algunos huevos cocidos conmigo porque creía que iba a tener hambre.
6. Él le dijo a ella que la quería mucho, ¿verdad?
7. ¿Para qué estás viviendo en México?
8. Si trabajas mucho, te vas a hacer rico dentro de unos pocos años, ¿verdad?
9. ¿Con quién fue al cine?
10. Yo no lo vi en el cine tampoco.

EXERCISE 16
Dictado

1. He couldn't stop and talk to us because he was in a hurry.
2. What are you wearing your new dress for?
3. Where are your parents from?
4. He said he was from Texas, didn't he?
5. Are you too busy to see me now?
6. Does anyone have any books that I can read?
7. You don't have to work up to four o'clock every day, do you?
8. I didn't see him at the movies either.
9. Go to the store and get some milk while I set the table.
10. As we were leaving, she said, "Please come back again".

EXERCISE 17
Conversación. *Conteste las siguientes preguntas.*

1. Where are you from?
2. Where did you come from?
3. What state are you from?
4. Who did you come with?
5. Who are you waiting for?
6. What are you looking at?
7. What are you looking for?
8. What are you laughing at?
9. What are you listening to?
10. What are you putting on?
11. Who are you talking to?
12. What are you talking about?
13. What are you thinking of (about)?

Conteste las siguientes preguntas en afirmativo y en negativo.

14. Did they look everywhere?
15. Did they go anywhere?
16. Did he ask any questions?
17. Did she take any books?
18. Did they bring any apples?
19. Does he live with anybody?
20. Do you want anything?
21. Do you need anything?
22. Did you go out of town yesterday?
23. Did he go out of town last month?
24. Is he out of town?
25. Was he out of town?

Lesson 20

VOCABULARY

1. **to break, broke** romper, rompió
2. **to try, tried** tratar, trató; probar, probó (*de intentar*)
3. **to drop, dropped** tirar, tiró; caérsele a uno, se le cayó a uno
4. **to pick out, picked out** escoger, escogió
5. **to pick up, picked up** alzar, alzó; recoger, recogió
6. **to reach reached** alcanzar, alcanzó; llegar, llegó
7. **strong** fuerte
8. **short** corto, chaparro
9. **black** negro
10. **crow** cuervo
11. **pitcher** jarra
12. **woods** bosque
    forest bosque
13. **stone** piedra
    rock roca
14. **way** manera; camino
15. **idea** idea
16. **top** parte superior; cima
17. **cream** crema
18. **sugar** azúcar
19. **potatoes** papas
20. **head** cabeza

IDIOMS

1. **to give up** darse por vencido
2. **to get thirsty, hungry, sleepy, etc.**
   darle a uno sed, hambre, sueño, etc.
   He got thirsty. Le dio a él sed.

LESSON 20

3. **more than anything else** más que nada, por encima de todo
4. **There is (are)... left.** Hay... Queda(n)...
   There's one left. Queda uno.
   There are three left. Quedan tres.
5. **to have... left** quedársele a uno...
   I have one left. Me queda uno.
   He has three left. Le quedan a él tres.
6. **not... any more, not... any longer** ya no
   I don't work here any more. Ya no trabajo aquí.
   I don't live in Mexico any longer. Ya no vivo en México.
7. **plenty (of)** bastante (*de sobrar*)
   I have plenty. Tengo bastante.
   I have plenty of time. Tengo bastante tiempo.
   (*Se emplea* **of** *sólo cuando sigue un sustantivo*).
8. **enough** suficiente, bastante (*de alcanzar*)
   enough time suficiente tiempo, bastante tiempo
   tall enough bastante alto
   (*se emplea* **enough** *antes de los sustantivos y después de los adjetivos y adverbios*).
9. **a great deal (of)** mucho   ⎧ *Éstos deben usarse en afirmativo en*
   a lot (of) mucho, muchos   ⎨ *vez de* **much**. *También pueden em-*
   lots (of) mucho, muchos   ⎩ *plearse en negativo e interrogativo.*

   (Se emplea **of** sólo cuando sigue un sustantivo. **A great deal (of)** se usa solamente con o al referirse a un sustantivo en singular).

EXERCISE 1
Traduzca las siguientes oraciones y practique leyéndolas

1. It's cold, isn't it?
2. It isn't cold, is it?
3. It was warm, wasn't it?
4. It wasn't warm, was it?
5. It's going to be cold, isn't it?

6. It isn't going to be cold, is it?
7. It was going to be warm, wasn't it?
8. It wasn't going to be warm, was it?
9. You're hungry, aren't you?
10. You aren't hungry, are you?
11. You were hungry, weren't you?
12. You weren't hungry, were you?
13. You're going to be hungry, aren't you?
14. You aren't going to be hungry, are you?
15. Where are you coming from?
16. What are you looking at?
17. What were you looking at?

Aprenda estas palabras.

1. **to fill, filled** llenar, llenó
2. **to complete, completed** completar, completó
3. **to translate, translated** traducir, tradujo
4. **to place, placed** colocar, colocó
5. **to practice, practiced** practicar, practicó
6. **to pronounce, pronounced** pronunciar, pronunció
7. **to change, changed** cambiar, cambió
8. **to form, formed** formar, formó
9. **to dictate, dictated** dictar, dictó
10. **sentence** oración
11. **phrase** frase
12. **blank** espacio
13. **idiom** modismo
14. **vocabulary** vocabulario
15. **auxiliary** auxiliar
16. **conversation** conversación
17. **infinitive** infinitivo
18. **adjective** adjetivo
19. **possessive adjetive** adjetivo posesivo
20. **adverb** adverbio
21. **verb** verbo
22. **noun** sustantivo
23. **pronoun** pronombre
24. **objective pronoun** pronombre objetivo
25. **possessive pronoun** pronombre posesivo
26. **preposition** preposición
27. **singular** singular

28. **plural** plural
29. **English** inglés
30. **correct** correcto
31. **following** siguiente
32. **number** número
33. **affirmative** afirmativo
34. **negative** negativo
35. **interrogative** interrogativo
36. **tense** tiempo
37. **present tense** tiempo presente
38. **past tense** tiempo presente
39. **future tense** tiempo futuro
40. **adverb of frequency** adverbio de frecuencia
41. **homework** tarea (*de escuela*)
42. **exercise** ejercicio
43. **page** página
44. **dictation** dictado

EXERCISE 2
Lea y traduzca las siguientes oraciones.

1. Fill the blanks with the correct preposition and translate.
2. Pronounce the past tense of these verbs.
3. Study the present tense of these verbs.
4. Read and translate the following sentences.
5. Study these phrases. Change them to the negative, interrogative, and interrogative negative.
6. Write the following sentences in English.
7. Learn the following idioms.
8. In English, adjectives are placed before nouns.
9. English adjectives have no singular or plural.
10. Fill the blanks with the correct form of the verb.
11. Learn the objective pronouns.
12. After the auxiliary can, we use the infinitive without to.
13. We're going to practice the verbs.
14. We're going to have conversation.
15. I'm going to dictate these sentences.

EXERCISE 3
Coloque los adverbios de frecuencia en el lugar correcto y traduzca.

1. (ever) Didn't they see a goose that laid a golden egg?
2. (seldom) He sleeps for two hours in the afternoon.
3. (always) Could they bring their dog with them?
4. (never) He can find what he's looking for.
5. (ever) Did you see so many people?
6. (usually) Does he bring his wife and family with him?
7. (rarely) I saw him before supper.
8. (sometimes) Why does he wait for her?
9. (always) She was looking at that picture on the wall.
10. (ever) I can't pronounce his name.

EXERCISE 4
Llene los espacios con la palabra correcta y traduzca. (Recuerde que **many** *y* **few** *se emplean antes de los sustantivos en plural y* **much** *y* **little** *antes de los sustantivos en singular.)*

1. (many, much) _____ people had cars, but (few, little) _____ used them every day.
2. How (many, much) _____ apples did you buy?
3. Please give me a (little, few) _____ more coffee.
4. Do you want a (little, few) _____ more sugar and cream?
5. Don't eat (much, many) _____ food before you go to bed.
6. I don't know why you brought so (many much) _____ eggs.
7. Do you have to learn (many, much) _____ verbs tomorrow?
8. (few, little) _____ children were sick the day before yesterday.
9. I have very (few, little) _____ work to do.
10. How (many, much) _____ time do you need?

EXERCISE 5
Llene los espacios con el pronombre posesivo que corresponde a las palabras entre paréntesis y traduzca.

1. I don't like my new suit, but I like (his new suit) _____.
2. He ate his apple, and she ate (her apple) _____.
3. She lost her notebook, so we gave her (our notebook) _____.
4. We wore our hats, and they wore (their hats).
5. This book is (my book) _____.
6. That book is (your book) _____.
7. My saint's day is in June. When is (your saint's day) _____?
8. If you don't have a pen, you can use (my pen) _____.
9. I don't want to use (her book) _____.
10. I want to use (my book) _____.

EXERCISE 6
Llene los espacios con **any, some, no, none** *y traduzca.*

1. Did you find _____ potatoes in the kitchen?
2. No, I didn't find _____ potatoes, but I found _____ bread.
3. Are you looking for _____ English teachers now?
4. Yes, I'm looking for _____ English teachers, but I don't want _____ who aren't American.
5. Are you going to buy _____ dresses when you go to the United States?
6. Yes, I'm going to buy _____ dresses and _____ shoes, but I'm not going to buy _____ hats.
7. I have _____ money. (*negativo*)
8. Did you say that you didn't have _____ money?
9. I said that I have _____. (*negativo*)
10. He took _____ money. (*negativo*) He took _____. (*negativo*)

LESSON 20

EXERCISE 7

Llene los espacios con **anything, something, nothing** *y traduzca.*

1. Do you want _____ for your birthday?
2. No, don't give me _____ for my birthday, but you can give me _____ for my saint's day.
3. I bought _____ for your birthday. (*afirmativo*)
4. I didn't know that you had enough money to buy _____.
5. There was _____ that we could do. (*negativo*)
6. There was _____ that we could do. (*afirmativo*)
7. They said _____. (*negativo*)
8. I'm going to tell you _____. (*afirmativo*)
9. Don't say _____.
10. I said _____. (*negativo*)

EXERCISE 8

Llene los espacios con **anybody (anyone), somebody (someone), nobody (no one)** *y traduzca.*

1. Did _____ call me this afternoon?
2. No, _____ called you this afternoon, but _____ called you this morning.
3. Don't tell _____.
4. _____ called you. (*negativo*)
5. _____ called you. (*afirmativo*)
6. I want to talk to _____ about this book.
7. There's _____ here now. (*negativo*)
8. I'm looking for _____ who can speak English.
9. There's _____ here who can speak English. (*negativo*)
10. There isn't _____ here who can speak English.

EXERCISE 9

Llene los espacios con **anywhere (any place), somewhere (some place), nowhere (no place)** *y traduzca.*

1. John often invited us _____.
2. John never invited us _____.
3. Did John ever invite us _____?
4. John rarely invited us _____.
5. Let's invite John _____.
6. Can I buy this _____?
7. I want to lie down _____ and go to sleep.
8. He's always going _____.
9. No one went _____ on Friday.
10. Take me _____ on Sunday.

EXERCISE 10

Llene los espacios y traduzca.

1. Did you speak to (todos) _____?
2. The children wanted to break (todo) _____.
3. Are you going to look (por todos lados) _____?
4. (Todo el mundo) _____ put on his hat.
5. Did she drop (todo) _____?
6. It's very hot (por todas partes) _____.
7. (Todos) _____ has to bring something.
8. Did (todos) _____ see (todo) _____?
9. Did they look for him (por todas partes) _____?
10. Is there room for (todos) _____?

EXERCISE 11

Llene los espacios con la forma correcta de los verbos **say** *o* **tell** *y traduzca.*

1. I'm going _____ you something on Sunday afternoon.
2. Don't _____ anything.
3. He _____ me that he couldn't understand what the teacher was _____.
4. I know she understood what I _____ because I _____ her in Spanish.
5. What are you going _____ him?
6. What are you going _____ them?
7. They didn't want _____ good-bye.
8. Please _____ the teacher that I can't come to school today.
9. What is that man _____?
10. He's _____ us that he can't hear.

EXERCISE 12

Traduzca al español.

1. How much money do you have left?
2. They had none left.
3. I don't have any left.
4. He has some apples left.
5. Is there a lot of money left?
6. Do you have anything left to eat?
7. Isn't there any food left?
8. How much money did you have left after you bought that suit?
9. I didn't have any money left after I bought that suit.
10. Is there any time left?

EXERCISE 13

*Traduzca las siguientes preguntas. Contéstelas en negativo, colocando **any more** y **any longer** al final de la oración.*

Por regla general se coloca **any more** y **any longer** al final de la oración.

1. Don't you love me any more?
2. Don't you work there any more?
3. Doesn't he live there any more?
4. Doesn't she see him any more?
5. Don't you study English any more?
6. Don't you go to school any longer?
7. Doesn't she teach Spanish any longer?
8. Doesn't she like Mexico any longer?
9. Don't they go to the movies any longer?
10. Don't you write to them any longer?

EXERCISE 14

Lea los siguientes números y fechas.

one hundred cien **one million**
one thousand mil un millón (de)

103	500	25,000	1st floor	April 17, 1947
105	505	50,000	2nd floor	May 5, 1842
110	550	75,000	3rd floor	February 14,
113	575	1,580,000	4th floor	1512
150	595	3,100,000	5th floor	November 3,
200	1,000	142nd Street	6th floor	1603
201	1,003	58th Street	7th floor	July 4, 1776
211	1,005	23rd Street	8th floor	
261	10,000	72nd Street	9th floor	
271	15,000	81st Street	10th floor	

Ortografía

1. Cuando un verbo termina en **y**, precedida por una consonante, se cambia la **y** por **i** y se le agrega **es** para formar la tercera persona singular del presente. Ejemplos: **he studies** *pero*: **he plays** (precedido por una vocal).
2. Cuando un verbo termina en sonido de **s**, **sh**, **ch**, **x**, se le agrega **es** para formar la tercera persona singular. Ejemplos: **kiss** (besar), **kisses**; **wash**, **washes**; **reach**, **reaches**; **fix**, **fixes**.
3. Cuando un verbo termina en **y**, precedida por una consonante, se cambia por **i** y se le agrega **ed** para formar el pasado. Ejemplos: **he hurried**; *pero*; **he played** (precedido por una vocal).
4. Los sustantivos terminados en **y**, precedida por una consonante, forman su plural cambiando la **y** por **i** y agregando la terminación **es**. Ejemplos: **city, cities family, families**.
5. Los sustantivos terminados en **s, sh, ch, x** forman su plural agregando **es**. Ejemplos: **dress, dresses fox, foxes**.
6. Los sustantivos terminados en **fe** forman su plural cambiando la **f** por **v** y agregando **es**. Ejemplos: **wife, wives knife, knives**. Muchos sustantivos terminados en **f** forman su plural cambiando la **f** por **v** y agregando **es**. Ejemplo: **loaf loaves**.
7. Si el verbo termina en **e**, ésta se suprime antes de agregar **ing**. Ejemplos: **give, giving come, coming**.
   Los verbos monosílabos que terminan en una sola consonante, precedida de una sola vocal, duplicarán la consonante final antes de agregar **ing**. Ejemplos: **put, putting stop, stopping**. Esta regla se aplicará también a los verbos polisílabos cuando la última sílaba lleva el acento. Ejemplo: **begin, beginning** *pero*: **visit, vistiting** (lleva el acento en la primera sílaba).
8. Los verbos monosílabos que terminan en una sola consonante, precedida de una sola vocal, duplicarán la consonante final antes de agregar **ed**. Ejemplos: **drop, dropped stop, stopeed**. Esta regla se aplicará también a los verbos polisílabos cuando la última sílaba lleva el acento. Ejemplos: **refer** (referir), **referred** *pero*: **visit, visited** (lleva el acento en la primera sílaba).

Todos los verbos regulares que duplican la consonante final para formar el gerundio sufren el mismo cambio en la formación del pasado. Ejemplos: **drop, dropping, dropped stop, stopping, stopped.**

EXERCISE 15

Escriba el plural de estos sustantivos.

1. city _____
2. country _____
3. boy _____
4. fox _____
5. family _____
6. birthday _____
7. way _____
8. dress _____
9. day _____
10. wife _____
11. knife _____
12. loaf _____

Escriba la tercera persona singular de estos verbos.

1. study _____
2. try _____
3. play _____
4. buy _____
5. hurry _____

Escriba el pasado de estos verbos. En algunos se duplica la consonante final antes de agregar **ed**. *En otros se cambia la* **y** *por* **i** *antes de agregar* **ed**. *A otros solamente se les agrega* **ed** *o* **d**.

1. drop _____
2. look _____
3. jump _____
4. pick out _____
5. study _____
6. live _____
7. hurry _____
8. turn off _____
9. play _____
10. listen (to) _____
11. try _____
12. form _____
13. walk _____
14. stop _____
15. wait (for) _____
16. answer _____

Escriba el gerundio de estos verbos. A algunos se le suprime la **e**, *a algunos se le duplica la consonante final, y a otros solamente se les agrega* **ing**.

1. run _____
2. play _____
3. be _____
4. try _____
5. get _____
6. help _____
7. drop _____
8. think _____
9. clean _____
10. turn on _____
11. do _____
12. live _____
13. stop _____
14. go _____
15. have _____
16. sleep _____
17. give _____
18. reply _____
19. take _____
20. write _____

EXERCISE 16
Práctica verbal

1. I always break the eggs.
2. I don't always break the eggs.
3. Do I ever break the eggs?
4. Don't I ever break the eggs?
5. Why don't I ever break the eggs?
6. I broke the pitcher.
7. I didn't break the pitcher.
8. Did I break the pitcher?
9. Didn't I break the pitcher?
10. Why didn't I break the pitcher?
11. I'm breaking everything.
12. I'm not breaking everything.
13. Am I breaking everything?
14. Am I not breaking everything?
15. Why am I breaking everything?
16. I was breaking something.
17. I wasn't breaking anything.
18. Was I breaking anything?
19. Wasn't I breaking anything?

20. What was I breaking?
21. I can break it.
22. I can't break it.
23. Can I break it?
24. Can't I break it?
25. Why can't I break it?
26. I could break these plates.
27. I couldn't break these plates.
28. Could I break these plates?
29. Couldn't I break these plates?
30. Why couldn't I break these plates?
31. I like to break them.
32. I don't like to break them.
33. Do I like to break them?
35. Why don't I like to break them?

EXERCISE 17

Práctica verbal. *Repita el ejercicio 16, usando formas de los verbos* **try, drop, give up, pick up, pick out, reach, get thirsty (sleepy, hungry, cold, etc.)** *en oraciones cortas. Emplee un sustantivo o pronombre distinto con cada verbo. Use las palabras interrogativas* **why** *y* **where** *cuando sea posible.*

EXERCISE 18

Lea y traduzca.

The crow and the pitcher

A crow, walking through the woods on a very hot day, got so thirsty that he wanted a drink of water more than anything else.

He was very happy when he found a pitcher under a tree; but, when he looked in the pitcher, he saw that it had only a little water left in it.

He tried to put his head through the mouth of the pitcher and reach the water with his bill, but the mouth was so small that he couldn't put his head through it.

Then the crow tried to break the pitcher, but he wasn't strong enough. "I can reach the water", he said, "but I have to think of a way first".

So the crow sat down and thought. He was almost ready to give up when he had an idea. There were a lot of little stones around the pitcher, and the crow thought of a way to use these stones to help him get the water.

He picked up a stone in his bill and dropped it into the pitcher. Then he picked up another and another and dropped them into the pitcher.

After a while the water reached the top of the pitcher, and the crow drank all the water.

EXERCISE 19
Escriba en inglés.

1. A él le gusta dormir más que nada.
2. Les di a ellos mucho dinero el martes, pero hoy les queda muy poco.
3. Prueba otra vez. No te des por vencido ahora.
4. Ellos trajeron mucha comida y había suficiente para todos.
5. ¿A alguien le dio sed mientras ellos estaban caminando?
6. Lo siento, pero ya no te quiero.
7. Escogimos muchas cosas para los niños, ¿verdad?
8. Tampoco estudió el hermano de Juan.
9. A mi abuelita le quedan solamente unos pocos años, y la quiero visitar más a menudo.
10. Aquella vaca negra no conoce el camino del granero.

EXERCISE 20
Dictado

1. Do you like a lot of cream and sugar in your coffee?
2. I like plenty of sugar but very little cream.
3. We have a great deal of time. Do you want to go to the movies?
4. No, I don't like the movies any more. I want to sleep for a few minutes if we have enough time left.
5. He tried three times and then gave up.
6. I'm going to take some water because I have an idea that it's going to be very hot.
7. We got so thirsty that we had to drink that dirty water.
8. Don't drop those rocks on the floor.
9. How much money did you have left after you bought your books?
10. Did everybody have enough time to finish?

EXERCISE 21
Conversación. *Conteste las siguientes preguntas.*

1. Do you have a great deal of time to study?
2. Do you drink a great deal of water?
3. Does he speak a lot of English?
4. Do you write a lot of letters?
5. Do you drink a lot of coffee?
6. Do you eat lots of candy?
7. Are there lots of factories on this street?
8. Does she have enough money?
9. Is the table big enough?
10. Do you have plenty?
11. Is there plenty of time?

Constete las siguientes preguntas en negativo.

12. Don't your speak English any longer?
13. Don't you live close to the school any longer?
14. Don't you need my book any more?
15. Don't you listen to the radio any more?
16. Don't you help your mother any more?
17. Don't you teach English any more?

Conteste las siguientes preguntas en afirmativo y en negativo.

18. Do you have any bread left?
19. Is there any butter left?
20. Do we have any meat left?
21. Do you see anything?
22. Do you hear anything?
23. Did he go any place?
24. Did you see anybody?
25. Did you visit anybody?

Vocabulary
English-Spanish

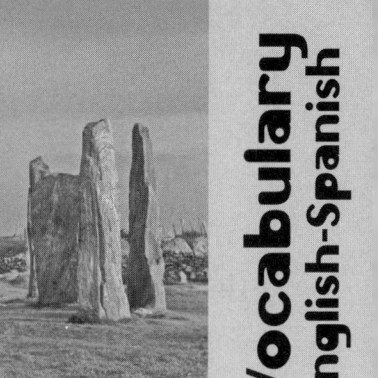

A

a un, uno, una
about acerca de, de; como; aproximadamente
above arriba (de) arriba de
across al otro lado de
adjective adjetivo
adverb adverbio
affirmative afirmativo
afraid: to be very afraid of tener (mucho) miedo a, de
after después (de que)
afternoon tarde
again otra vez, de nuevo
all todo (a, os, as)
almost casi
always siempre
am: I am soy, yo estoy
American estadounidense
among entre
an un, uno, una
and y
angry enojado
animal animal
another otro
(to) answer contestar
answered
answered
any algún; alguno(s)
   not... any no... ninguno(s)
anybody alguien; cualquiera
   not... anybody no... nadie
anyone alguien; cualquiera
   not... anyone no... nadie
any place alguna parte; cualquier lugar
   not... any place no... ninguna parte
anything algo; cualquier cosa
   not... anything no... nada
anywhere alguna parte; cualquier lugar
   not... anywhere no... ninguna parte
apple manzana

April abril
around alrededor de
as mientras, cuando
(to) ask preguntar: **to ask a question** hacer una pregunta; **to ask about** preguntar por
    asked
    asked

(to) ask pedir (*a alguien*)
    asked
    asked
(to) ask for pedir (*algo*)
    asked for
    asked for
asleep dormido (*profundamente*)
at a; en
aunt tía
auxiliary auxiliar

B

bad malo
barn granero
bathroom baño
(to) be ser; estar
    was, were
    been
(to) be about tratar de
    was, were about
    been about
beautiful bello, hermoso
because porque
(to) become llegar a ser, hacerse, volverse, ponerse
    became
    became
bed cama
bedroom recámara
before antes de
(to) begin empezar
    began
    begun
behind detrás de

beside al lado de
besides además (de)
between entre
big grande; alto
bill billete; cuenta; pico (*de ave*)
birthday cumpleaños
black negro
blanks espacios
blue azul
book libro
both ambos
boy muchacho
bread pan; **a loaf of bread** un pan (*de caja*)
(to) break romper
    broke
    broken
breakfast desayuno
(to) bring traer
    brought
    brought
brother hermano

brown color café
busy ocupado
but pero, sino
butter mantequilla

(to) buy comprar
    bought
    bought
by por, frente a

C

cake pastel
(to) call llamar
    called
    called
can poder
candy dulce
car coche
chair silla
(to) change cambiar
    changed
    changed
child niño, niña; hijo, hija
children niños, niñas; hijos, hijas
city ciudad
clean limpio
(to) clean limpiar
    cleaned
    cleaned
close (to) cerca (de)
(to) close cerrar
    closed
    closed
coffee café (*bebida*)
cold frío; catarro; **I'm (very) cold** tengo (mucho) frío; **I have a cold** tengo catarro; **it's (very) cold** hace (mucho) frío

colony colonia (*población*)
(to) come venir
    came
    come
(to) come back regresar (*de allá para acá*)
    came back
    come back
comfortable cómodo
(to) complete completar
    completed
    completed
conversation conversación
(to) correct corregir
    corrected
    corrected
could pudo, podía
country país, campo
cousin primo
cow vaca
cream crema
crow cuervo
cup taza
curtain cortina
(to) cut cortar
    cut
    cut

D

daughter hija
day día; **the day after tomorrow** pasado mañana; **the day before yesterday** antier
December diciembre
desk escritorio
(to) dictate dictar
    dictated
    dictated
dining room comedor
dinner comida principal
dirty sucio

(to) do hacer
    did
    done
doctor doctor
dog perro
dollar dólar
door puerta
down abajo
dress vestido
(to) drink beber
    drank
    drunk
(to) drop tirar, caérsele a uno
    dropped
    dropped

E

each cada
early temprano
easy fácil
(to) eat comer
    ate
    eaten
egg huevo
eight ocho
eighteen dieciocho
eighty ochenta
eleven once
English inglés
enough suficiente

ever alguna vez, a veces; **not... ever** nunca
every cada
everywhere (every place) por, a, en todas partes
everybody todo el mundo, todos
everything todo, todas las cosas
exercise ejercicio
eye ojo

F

factory fábrica
family familia
far (from) lejos (de)
farm granja
farmer granjero
fast rápido; aprisa
father padre, papá
February febrero
(to) feel sentir
    felt
    felt
fence cerca, barda
few pocos
field campo
fifteen quince
fifth quinto
fifty cincuenta
(to) fill llenar
    filled
    filled
(to) find encontrar
    found
    found
fine bueno, muy bien
(to) finish acabar, terminar
    finished
    finished

first primero
five cinco
(to) fix arreglar
    fixed
    fixed
floor piso, suelo
flower flor
following siguiente
food alimento
for para, por
forest bosque
(to) forget olvidar
    forgot
    forgotten
fork tenedor
(to) form formar
    formed
    formed
four cuatro
fourteen catorce
fourth cuarto
forty cuarenta
fox zorro
Friday viernes
friend amigo
from de

G

garage garaje; taller
garden jardín

gas gas
geese gansos

(to) get conseguir
    got
    got
(to) get angry (at) enojarse (con)
    got angry (at)
    got angry (at)
(to) get mad (at) enojarse; ponerse furiososo (con)
    got mad (at)
    got mad (at)
(to) get rich hacerse rico, enriquecerse
    got rich
    got rich
(to) get sleepy entrarle a uno sueño; estar soñoliento
    got sleepy
    got sleepy
(to) get to llegar a
    got to
    got to
(to) get here, there llegar
    got here, there
    got here, there
(to) get thirsty darle a uno sed
    got thirsty
    got thirsty
(to) get up levantarse
    got up
    got up

girl muchacha
(to) give dar; regalar
    gave
    given
(to) give up darse por vencido; renunciar
    gave up
    given up
glass vidrio; cristal; vaso
(to) go ir
    went
    gone
(to) go back regresar (*de acá para allá*)
    went back
    gone back
gold oro; de oro
golden de oro, dorado
good bueno
good-bye adiós
goose ganso, oca
(to) go out salir
    went out
    gone out
(to) go to bed acostarse
    went to bed
    gone to bed
(to) go to sleep dormirse
    went to sleep
    gone to sleep
grandfather abuelo
grandmother abuela
grandparents abuelos
green verde

H

happy feliz, contento
hard duro, difícil; mucho (*adv.*)
hat sombrero
(to) have tener, haber
   had
   had
hay heno
he él
head cabeza
(to) hear oír
   heard
   heard
hello hola
(to) help ayudar
   helped
   helped
her su (s) de ella; la (*pron. obj.*)
here aquí, acá
hers el suyo, los suyos (de ella)
him lo, le (*pron. obj.*)
his su (s) de él; el suyo, los suyos (de él)
home hogar, casa
homework tarea (*de escuela*)
hot caliente; **I'm (very) hot** tengo (mucho) calor; **it's (very) hot** hace (mucho) calor
hotel hotel
hour hora
house casa
how ¿cómo?
how many ¿cuántos?
how much ¿cuánto?
hundred: one hundred cien
(to be) hungry: to be (very) hungry tener (mucha) hambre
(to) hurry apresurarse
   hurried
   hurried
husband esposo

I

I yo
idea idea
idiom modismo
if si (*condicional*)
in en, dentro de
infinite infinitivo
in front of adelante de, enfrente de
interesting interesante
interrogative interrogativo
into al, en
(to) invite invitar
   invited
   invited
is es, está
it lo, la (*cosa o animal*)
its su (*cosa o animal*)

J

January enero
July Julio
June junio

(to) jump saltar, brincar
    jumped
    jumped

K

(to) kill matar
    killed
    killed
kind clase, tipo; amable
kitchen cocina

knife cuchillo
knives cuchillos
(to) know saber, conocer
    knew
    known

L

last último, pasado
last name apellido
last night anoche
last week la semana pasada
(to) laugh (at) reírse (de)
    laughed (at)
    laughed (at)
(to) lay eggs poner huevos
    laid eggs
    laid eggs
(to) learn aprender
    learned
    learned
(to) leave dejar; salir; marcharse; irse
    left
    left

(to) let dejar
    let
    let
letter carta; letra
(to) lie down recostarse
    lay down
    lain down
light luz; claro; ligero
(to) like gustar, simpatizar
    liked
    liked
(to) listen (to) escuchar
    listened (to)
    listened (to)
little pequeño, chico; poco
(to) live vivir
    lived
    lived

living room sala
long largo
(to) look (at) mirar; fijarse (en)
   looked (at)
   looked (at)
(to) look for buscar
   looked for
   looked for

(to) look out (of) asomarse (por)
   looked out (of)
   looked out (of)
(to) lose perder
   lost
   lost
(to) love amar, querer
   loved
   loved

M

mad enojado; furioso
(to) make hacer
   made
   made
man hombre, señor
manger pesebre
many muchos (as)
March marzo
May mayo
me me (*pron. obj.*)
meat carne (*comestible*)
(to) meet encontrar (se) (*personas*); conocer (*personas por primera vez*)
   met
   met
men hombres
metal metal
Mexican mexicano
Mexico México
milk leche

million millón (de)
mine el mío, la mía, los míos, las mías
minute minuto
Miss señorita (*con apellido o nombre*)
money dinero
month mes
more más
morning mañana
mother madre, mamá
mouth boca; pico; hocico
movie película
movies cine; películas
Mr. señor (*con apellido o nombre*)
Mrs. Señora (*con apellido o nombre*)
much mucho (a)
my mi (s)

N

name nombre
narrow estrecho, angosto
near cerca (de)
(to) need necesitar
    needed
    needed
negative negativo
never nunca, jamás
new nuevo
next próximo
next to junto a
nice bonito; simpático, agradable
night noche
nine nueve
nineteen diecinueve

ninety noventa
no no; ningún
nobody nadie, ninguna persona
none ninguno
no one nadie, ninguna persona
no place ninguna parte
not no
notebook cuaderno
nothing nada
noun sustantivo
November noviembre
now ahora
nowhere ninguna parte
number número

O

object complemento (*gramática*); objeto
October octubre
of de
office oficina
often a menudo
old viejo, anciano
on en, sobre
once una vez
one uno
only solamente; único
(to) open abrir
    opened
    opened

or o
other otro
our nuestro (a, os, as)
ours el nuestro, la nuestra, los nuestros, las nuestras
out afuera
out of fuera de
outside afuera, fuera de
over sobre, por, directamente encima de
over here para acá, hacia acá, por acá
over there para allá hacia allá, por allá

P

page página
parents padres
(to) pass pasar
    passed
    passed
past tense tiempo pasado
pen pluma
pencil lápiz
people gente
phone teléfono
phrase frase
(to) pick out escoger
    picked out
    picked out
picture cuadro, retrato; película
place lugar
(to) place colocar
    placed
    placed
plate plato

please por favor
plenty (of) bastante
prural plural
poor pobre
(to) put poner, meter
    put
    put
(to) put on ponerse
    put on
    put on
possessive posesivo
potato papa
(to) practice practicar
    practiced
    practiced
preposition preposición
present tense tiempo presente
pronoun pronombre
pronunciation pronunciación
pure puro

Q

question pregunta

R

rabbit conejo
race carrera; raza
radio radio
rarely rara vez
(to) reach llegar a; alcanzar
    reached
    reached

(to) read leer
    read
    read
ready listo
record player tocadiscos
red rojo

(to) reply contestar
    replied
    replied
  rich rico
  rock roca

room cuarto; lugar
(to) run correr
    ran
    run
  rug alfombra, tapete

S

sad triste
same mismo
Saturday sábado
saucer plato pequeño
    (*de taza*)
(to) say decir
    said
    said
  school escuela
  second segundo
(to) see ver
    saw
    seen
  seldom rara vez
  selfish (*adj.*) egoísta
(to) sell vender
    sold
    sold
  sentence oración
  September septiembre
(to) set poner
    set
    set
(to) set the table poner la
    mesa
    set the table
    set the table
  seven siete
  seventeen diecisiete

seventy setenta
shallow poco profundo
she ella
shoe zapato
short corto; chaparrro
(to) show enseñar; mostrar
    showed
    showed
  sick enfermo
  singular singular
  sister hermana
(to) sit (down) sentarse
    sat (down)
    sat (down)
  six seis
  sixteen dieciséis
  sixty sesenta
(to) sleep dormirse
    slept
    slept
  sleepy: to be (very) sleepy
    tener (mucho) sueño
  slow lento, despacio
  slowly lentamente
  small pequeño, chico
  so así es que; para que;
    por lo tanto; tan
  so much tanto
  so many tantos

some algún, alguno (s)
somebody alguien, alguna persona
someone alguien, alguna persona
some place alguna parte
something algo, alguna cosa
sometimes algunas veces
somewhere alguna parte
son hijo
soon pronto
soup sopa
Spanish español
(to) speak hablar, platicar
    spoke
    spoken
spoon cuchara
(to) stand up pararse
    stood up
    stood up
(to) start empezar
    started
    started
state estado
stone piedra
(to) stop detener (se)
    stopped
    stopped
store tienda
stork cigüeña
story cuento
stove estufa
street calle
strong fuerte
student alumno, estudiante
(to) study estudiar
    studied
    studied
sugar azúcar
suit traje
Sunday domingo
supper cena, merienda
sweet dulce

T

table mesa
(to) take llevar, tomar
    took
    taken
(to) take off quitarse
    took off
    taken off
(to) take out sacar
    took out
    taken out
(to) talk hablar; platicar
    talked
    talked
tall alto
(to) teach enseñar
    taught
    taught
teacher profesor
telephone teléfono

(to) tell decir, contar
    told
    told
ten diez
thanks gracias
that que; lo que, ese, esa; aquel, aquella; eso, aquello
that one ése, ésa; aquél, aquélla
theirs el suyo, los suyos (de ellos o ellas)
them los, las (*pron. obj.*)
then entonces; después
there allí, allá
there is (*sing.*) hay
there are (*plural*) hay
there was (*sing.*) había, hubo
there were (*plural*) había, hubo
these estos, estas; éstos, éstas
they ellos, ellas
thing cosa
(to) think pensar, creer
    thought
    thought
(to) think about (of) pensar en
    thought about (of)
    thought about (of)
third tercero
thirsty: to be (very) thirsty tener (mucha) sed
this este, esta; esto

this one éste, ésta
those esos, esas; aquellos, aquellas; ésos, ésas; aquéllos, aquéllas
thousand mil
three tres
thirteen trece
through por, a través de
Thursday jueves
time tiempo; hora; vez
tired cansado
to a; hasta
today hoy
tomorrow mañana
tonight esta noche
too también; demasiado
too much demasiado
too many demasiados
top parte superior
toward hacia
(to) translate traducir
    translated
    translated
tree árbol
(to) try tratar, probar
    tried
    tried
Tuesday martes
(to) turn off apagar, cerrar, parar
    turned off
    turned off
(to) turn on poner, encender, prender, abrir
    turned on
    turned on

turtle tortuga
twelve doce
twenty veinte
twenty-one veintiuno

twenty-two veintidós
two dos
two hundred doscientos

U

uncle tío
under debajo de
(to) understand entender
    understood
    understood
United States Estados Unidos

until hasta
up arriba, hacia arriba
up to hasta
(to) use usar
    used
    used
usually usualmente

V

vase florero
very muy
(to) visit visitar

visited
visited
vocabulary vocabulario

W

(to) wait (for) esperar
    waited (for)
    waited (for)
(to) wake up despertar (se)
    woke up
    woke up
(to) walk caminar
    walked
    walked

wall pared
(to) want querer
    wanted
    wanted
warm caliente; **I'm (very) warm** tengo (mucho) calor; **it's (very) warm** hace (mucho) calor

(to) wash lavar (se)
    washed
    washed
(to) watch TV ver television
    watched TV
    watched TV
water agua
way manera, modo
we nosotros
weak débil
(to) wear llevar (*ropa o joyería*)
    wore
    worn
Wednesday miércoles
week semana
well bien
what ¿qué?; lo que, que
when cuándo, cuando
where dónde, donde
which qué; ¿cuál?, que, cual
while rato; mientras que
white blanco

who ¿quién?; ¿quiénes?
whom prep. + quién
why ¿por qué?
wife esposa
(to) win ganar (*de jugar*)
    won
    won
window ventana
with con
without sin
woman mujer, señorita, señora
women mujeres
wood madera
woods bosque (s)
word palabra
(to) work trabajar
    worked
    worked
(to) write escribir
    wrote
    written

Y

yard patio; espacio que rodea una casa
year año
yes sí
yesterday ayer
you tú, usted, ustedes
young joven
young man (el) joven
young woman (la) joven

your su (s) (*de usted o de ustedes*)
yours el tuyo, la tuya, los tuyos, las tuyas: el suyo, la suya, los suyos, las suyas (*de usted o de ustedes*)